# EVE, OUR MYTHIC MOTHER
## Exposing the Lies of Patriarchy

Patricia Lynn Reilly

Author: Patricia Lynn Reilly, M.Div.
Publishing Support: Monette Chilson
Cover Image: Cissie Watson
Cover Design: Monica Rodgers
Printed in the United States of America
Purchase book at www.JoinTheReclamation.com

## Advance Praise 1

"Patricia's book is beautifully written, engaging and compelling. She is a gentle teacher and healer. She touches painful areas with such tenderness and care, and leaves behind healing and hope. She has a deep understanding of religion and the issues that so many of us have struggled with, wondered about, and cursed. Patricia guides us through the past into the present with research, stories, compassion, thoughtful examples, and ways to heal and grow. Although I have done quite a bit of reading on the topic of women and religion, Patricia gave me new ideas and helped me see old thoughts in new ways by providing fresh perspectives and by nudging me to think further and more broadly." —*Linda Bengston, Retired Editor*

# EVE, OUR MYTHIC MOTHER
## Exposing the Lies of Patriarchy

## Book Description

Once Patricia realized that Eve the Mother of All Living was demoted by men to become the queen-pin of patriarchy's assault on womankind, she made a promise to reclaim Eve's truth by exposing patriarchy's lies. The promise empowered her to claim the theological and intellectual authority necessary to dismantle, story by story, the patriarchal infrastructure that demoted Eve and then used her reworked story to deny women sovereignty over their own bodies and lives.

## Advance Praise 2

Reading *"Eve, Our Mythic Mother* will deepen your understanding of the foundational flaw in the Genesis mythology conveyed in the scriptures and storybooks of our childhoods. If you are ready to ditch the shame and blame wrongfully assigned to girls and women through the misogynistic twisting of Eve's story, receive the Eve's challenge to bite into your life and fullness of its possibility." —Monette Chilson, Author of *Sophia Rising;* Founder of WomanSpirit Reclamation

"On a humanitarian level, my heart breaks seeing how sacred texts like the Bible are still used globally to sanction all sorts of harmful practices and beliefs which shame, blame, and stigmatize the female body. I highly recommend Patricia Lynn Reilly's latest book *Eve, our Mythic Mother: Exposing the Lies of Patriarchy* for anyone seeking to shed the patriarchal baggage written into the Adam and Eve story and/or wanting to reclaim Eve as a powerful and life-giving Mother of all Living to include in a self-defined spirituality." —Emily Nielsen Jones, Founding Partner of the Imago Dei Fund and Author of The Girl Child & Her Long Walk to Freedom

"I listened to heavy metal this morning and it was therapeutic. I am at peace. This music got me through middle school and into high school. It is so centering, grounding, and powerful. I put this music away to become the person I believed society wanted me to be. I found myself again through the words of Eve. I could feel her presence stretch through my life before I had a name for her. She was there in the quiet spaces and in the loudest moments, holding space for my life to unfold, knowing I would come back to her truth and my own, one of these days." —Dominique Jean Baptiste, Community Coordinator at WomanSpirit Reclamation

"In taking the journey through *Eve, Our Mythic Mother: Exposing the Lies of Patriarchy*, Patricia offered me an opportunity to transform the image that was spoon-fed to us. Her use of poetry, story, and ritual opened new windows to myself and compelled me to extend a hand both backward—to my ancestors, and forward to my daughters, to reclaim what was rightfully ours to begin with: that our bodies are to be revered, that we are holy, and most of all that we are good." —Carrie Vidal, Therapist and Mother of 2 Daughters

## Author's Notes and Gratitude

### The Flow

*Eve, our Mythic Mother: Exposing the Lies of Patriarchy* flows from personal story to mythic excavation, from poetry to photographs, from deep breaths to pauses between chapters, from challenging lies (Chap. 1-4) to liberating truths (Chap. 5-8). The accumulation of patriarchy's lies can be difficult to explore. However, the gifts we receive from our courageous exploration are personal liberation and a woman-affirming panoramic view of women's mythic history.

### The Text

Clearly, spell-check has been tainted by patriarchy's preference for the male. It did not approve of my choice to demote "**g**od" to lowercase status nor my choice to elevate "**M**other" to uppercase prominence. Thus, spell-check flagged every such entry. It felt empowering to reject each of spell-check's corrections!

### Gratitude

EVE's Team of Readers: Thank you, Carrie, Dominique, Emily, and Linda for your essential feedback and suggestions.

EVE's Team of Cheerleaders: Thank you, D'Vorah, Marilyn, Monette, Monica, and Pat for your ongoing encouragement and belief in this project.

EVE's Painter: Thank you, Cissie Watson, for spending gracious, productive time in your studio with thoughts of EVE, that culminated in her image on the cover.

EVE's Champion: I am grateful to Emily Jones, author *of The Girl Child & Her Long Walk to Freedom*, who spearheaded the transformation of the book's "Encounter with Eve" into a video to be shared with girls and women around the world.

EVE's Circle of Mentors: I am grateful to all the female readers and writers quoted and acknowledged on these pages for telling the truth of a woman's life—a transformative truth, which set in motion the possibility of our liberation from patriarchy's lies.

### The Mythic Team

As you will read in Chapter 1, I consider Eve, Lilith, and Mary my Mythic Mothers. As I uncovered their stories, which intersect at crucial junctures in patriarchal history, they evolved into a powerful Trinity of inspiration, empowerment, and self-love. As I sorted through the lies to uncover the truth about their mythic evolution, they restored me to a loving relationship with myself. I am grateful that their truth truly does set us free.

*I dedicate this book to my mother*,
Kathleen Patricia Diehm Reilly (1927-1993).
Daughter of Catherine Tyndall Diehm,
Grand-daughter of Anna Neville Tyndall,
Great grand-daughter of Catherine Kelly Neville,
In gratitude for her ongoing inspiration.

Blessed are you among women, dear Mother.
I grieve your wounds.
I celebrate your courage.
I honor you in every word in this book.
Together we tell the untold stories of a lifetime.

# EVE, OUR MYTHIC MOTHER
*Exposing the Lies of Patriarchy*

_____

## Words Made Flesh

I love words. Words becoming flesh and feeling, sweat and sensation. Words opening mind, body, and memory. Words stimulating thought, inspiring action, changing lives. Words clarifying what's in, under, and around them. I like clarity, too. I don't like obscuration. I consider it a compliment when someone understands my words, when they say the meaning is apparent, not layered, not hidden, not requiring pursuit.

### Private Words

I've been writing simple, clear words since I was seven. Gathering my feeling, longing, and tears into words to my father 3,000 miles away. "I miss you, Daddy." Letters found tied with a ribbon in his lonely apartment after his death. Letters to my Nana and Mama while in the orphanage, reaching out to touch and remember them through words. Words written with my tears, received by theirs. Words, ever hopeful of reunion. _Shared tears. Shared hope. Words becoming flesh, the tie that binds, across the excruciating distance._

In high school, I wrote letters to the protestant god in response to my daily Bible readings. My words, longing for god to approve my choices, my beliefs, my zeal. "Father in heaven, hear my prayer, make me perfect, use me to change the world." God became flesh, they say. The word, logos, became flesh and dwelt among us. That which was indiscernible, out of reach, beyond pursuit, was born of flesh to become flesh. _From abstraction to fleshiness. From platforms and positions to vulnerability. From word to touch to sacred messiness, to life here and now, till death do us part._

At college, New Testament words circumscribed my intellectual pursuits and vocational interests: "Suffer not a woman to teach, not to usurp authority over the man. For Adam was formed first, then Eve." I was an anomaly, near the top of my class in an institution that denied full professorships to women. Men were the leaders and teachers. Women were the followers and students. No matter how successful I was, I remained ineligible to become a minister, theologian, or professor—the vocations for which I had been unintentionally groomed since childhood. _Like the steady drip of an IV inserted at birth, my dreams were silenced by the words absorbed into my life stream._

The Bible I read daily as a child, adolescent, and young adult was filled with men's words, stories, and interpretations of the divine. Two impulses arose within me during those years. The vulnerability of my status as orphan required that I learn the party line and conform to it.

Yet a deeper part of my being remained untouched by those words. That part of me was accumulating courage for the day when I would leave the suffocating world of fundamentalism and venture into the open spaces of a life-affirming spirituality. *This little light of mine, I'm going to let it shine. Won't let anyone blow it out!*

After college, I began to question god's words in the secret of my heart. They were harsh and restrictive. They denied the good within and around me. They divided the world into simplistic categories: good/bad; god/devil; believer/unbeliever; heaven/hell. I longed for words of welcome and celebration rather than words of warning and judgment. I longed for spaciousness, for more room around my thoughts and feelings, for deeper breaths, for playmates beyond the chosen, the elect, the predestined. An open window. *Blow, fresh air, blow into dusty rooms of old. Refresh and make new.*

My secret courage was nourished as I gathered an alternative scripture from the works of poets, artists, and writers. Given my early identification with men, Walt Whitman, Rainier Rilke, Chaim Potok, and Hermann Hesse were the first to feed my suspicion of the "Word of God." Unlike the rigid teachings of my childhood and adolescence, which imprisoned the divine and prescribed my responses, the life-affirming visions of these men employed open language and unfolding imagery. Their words deepened my longing to venture out beyond orthodoxy. Their images inspired my imagination.

I read Walt Whitman's *Leaves of Grass* in a secret corner of the Princeton Seminary library. I drank in his blasphemous words. They quenched my thirst for a language with which to celebrate myself without conditions, apologies, or disclaimers. Having just begun the journey through my intellectual, religious, and personal past, I wasn't ready to allow his words to form on my lips, yet they remained within me. Years later, my threefold journey completed, Whitman's words from "Song of Myself" became my first self-celebration. *I am larger, better than I thought. I did not know I held so much goodness.*

After graduation I continued my studies, claiming intellectual and theological equality with the gods of traditional religion and their sacred text, the Bible. The dethronement of the male god was a crucial task to complete on my journey. My imagination, intellect, and vision were freed of the shackles of a lifetime as his words and images were exorcised from my mind, heart, and body. *To know anything at all about our history, our bodies, ourselves, we must reach beyond what they told us, what they taught us, what they want from us. We must reach back to the very beginning.*

Grounded in my own life, supported by a circle of women, I was determined to give as many hours of attention, creativity, and support to women as I had given to men. That determination led me to develop a woman-affirming ministry and to design a business capable of holding the full range of my creative adventures. That determination also inspired me to write as many words in service of my own professional life as I had written to men and gods. I outlined several writing projects, secured an agent, and sold my first book to a publisher. Since then, I have written several more. *I imagine them as my daughters, born of my vow of faithfulness to myself.*

## Public Words

As an author I have never begun a project with a blank page. In my experience writing is more like gathering words, regularly turning toward them, and then crafting them to reach beyond, beneath, in back of themselves. Each idea, outline, and assignment begin with a ritual reading of my journals and writings for inspiration, for the kernel that will eventually become the chapter, article, keynote, lecture, performance piece, or book.

As the words travel from my journal (private musings rooted in the fleshiness of my tears, sweat, longing, and fear) to book, article, and lecture (public platforms and positions crafted for an audience), they are often drained of their personal vulnerability, of the messiness of ordinary life that gave birth to them in the first place. Yet underneath the public words, the private fleshiness pulsates: there she is, the abandoned girl, longing for her mother, heard in the reworked prayers of the feminist theologian: "Our Mother, who art within us;" there she is, the fearful girl, befriending the darkness of solitary confinement at the orphanage, heard in the priestess' tribute to Mother Darkness.

There she is, the fierce adolescent, wrestling for her place as a world-changer among the boys, heard in the iconoclast's challenge: "God the father has remained an undisturbed idol for too long;" and there she is, the troubled young woman, struggling to love and trust herself enough to come out of hiding with her calling, heard in the words of the WomanChurch minister: "It is right and good that you are woman." Listen deeply enough to any author's words and you will touch their personal vulnerability.

Once tossed to the winds as public writings, my words develop a life of their own. Some of them are used by others in their dissertations, published books, magazines, newsletters, web postings, and course readers. They are quoted by kindred spirits and by angry detractors. Some live quieter lives, remaining on the pages of my journal until now. In the fullness of time, musing becomes word becomes journal entry becomes public expression becomes flesh again in the experience of you, the reader. *Nothing has been lost or forgotten. In the roundabout way life works, all is re-membered, resurrected, re-constituted, re-enacted.*

## Blasphemous Words

And then there are the words about Eve. She was an essential part of the sacred drama that shaped my adolescence in the Protestant church. I never heard a positive word about her in Sunday School classes or Youth Group meetings. The words written about Eve, spoken about her from the pulpit, and expounded upon in Christian college classes inspired this book. Words about her fill volumes, and over the years I have come to believe that the words men wrote about her are among the most consequential and blasphemous words ever written.

*Consequential*, in that they catalogue the shift from pre-patriarchal, Goddess-centered, partnership-based community to monotheism and its violent demotion of the Mother Goddess and its equally violent elevation of "the one true male god."

*Blasphemous*, in that those words that fill volumes vilify the Goddess, reverse the truth about her life and legacy, and justified her genocide. They also shape the patriarchal indoctrination that generations of girls from around the world continue to be subjected to—indoctrination, convincing us of our secondary status in service of men.

I left no word unturned while searching for the pre-patriarchal truth about the women who were marginalized in the male-centered myths and scriptures of my early years. I knew my own marginalization and that of my Protestant mother and Catholic grandmother were connected to these Mythic Mothers and their treatment. For some of us, the deconstruction of the Bible's misogynistic myths and stories, and the reclamation of Eve are essential tasks in our unfolding. In fact, women have been biting into these misogynistic texts and re-interpreting them from a woman's perspective for over 1,700 years, reaching back to the Montanist women of the second century who claimed Eve as their champion.

Reclaiming Eve empowered me to claim the theological and intellectual authority necessary to dismantle, story by story, the patriarchal infrastructure that denies women sovereignty over their own bodies and lives. Reclaiming Eve in 2022 also means rising up in response to patriarchy's theocratic decision to criminalize abortion. And fueled by great urgency, reclaiming Eve means saying NO MORE to violence against women, including the murder of one of the world's women or girls by someone in her family every 11 minutes.

## An Introduction to Eve

Eve will tell her entire story later in the book. Here she will introduce herself as we begin excavating patriarchy's myths and mis-representations to unearth ancient truths. Truths that were intentionally twisted out of shape by the male god-makers and system-builders. Imagine hearing these words in the church or home of your childhood. Imagine Eve walking among us.

I was once known throughout the world as the Mother of All Living. The wisest among you have always honored me in your myths of beginnings. I have been called by many names, Fertile One Who Births All Things, The Great Mother, Law-Giving Mother, The Bearing One, She Who Gives Birth to the Gods, Queen of Heaven, True Sovereign, Mother of the World, Queen of the Stars. I was called Inanna in Ur; Ishtar in Babylon; Astarte in Phoenicia; Isis in Egypt; Womb Mother in Assyria, and Cerridwen among the Celts.

I was worshipped for many centuries before the god of the Hebrews was imagined into being. As men became threatened by my power and intimate involvement in the origins of all life, they swallowed my story into their unfolding mythologies and twisted my truth. My original power and glory are hardly recognizable in the stories you heard in the homes and churches of your childhood. The image of a father god ordering the world into being was firmly imprinted on your imaginations. *Did you even notice the absence of the Mother?*

As the Mother of all Living, I pick the good fruit of life. It is pleasant to the eye and offers well-being. It is wise and opens the way to self-discovery and understanding. Those among you who are curious, who lust for life in all its fluidity, dare with me. Bite into life and the fullness of its possibility. Take, eat of the good fruit of life. Open to the depths of goodness within you. Believe in your goodness. Celebrate your goodness. Live out of the abundance of who you are as a Child of Life. Affirm the original goodness of your children and your children's children until the stories of old hold no sway in their hearts.

*I am Eve, the Mother of All Living, culmination of creation.*
*I hold and nurture life within me.*
*In the fullness of time, I thrust and push life from me.*
*And all that I have given birth to is good, it is very good.*

Our journeys are unique and reflect our own life experience. Wherever you are on your reclamation journey, receive what deepens your self-love and self-understanding from this book and "with a breath of kindness blow the rest away."

**A Pause Between Chapters to Clarify Terms**
Theocracy/Autocracy: What's Eve Got to Do with It?

**Theocracy** is a form of government in which a deity or religious institution is the source from which all authority derives.

**Autocracy** is a form of government in which one person claims absolute power to rule. The autocrat may or may not claim that his ultimate authority comes from a god or a religion.

"There is a tsunami of national laws being pushed through in the USA right now. We are seeing a constant push for **theocracy**."
—Annie Laurie Gaylord, *Freedom from Religion Foundation*

"Since I moved to the United States from Egypt, I've been saying that the US is a **theocracy,** but no one is paying attention. The Christian right is more powerful than Egypt's Muslim Brotherhood ever dreamed of being. But because they are primarily white and Christian they are considered less dangerous."
—Mona Eltahwy, *The Seven Deadly Sin for Women and Girls*

"Women's political power is essential to a properly functioning multiracial democracy, and **fully free, empowered women are a threat to autocracy**. Assaults on women's and LGBTQ+ rights—and attempts to put women "in their place"—constitute a backlash against feminist progress expanding women's full inclusion in public life."
—Zoe Marks and Erica Chenoweth, "The Patriarchs' War on Women" (MS. Magazine)

"Reclaiming Eve in 2022 means rising up in response to patriarchy's theocratic decision to criminalize abortion and its threat to criminalize contraception. And fueled by great urgency, reclaiming Eve means saying **NO MORE** to violence against women, including the rape and incest of our daughters and the murder of one of the world's women or girls by someone in her own family every 11 minutes."
—Patricia Lynn Reilly, Humanist Author and Chaplain

# CHAPTER 1

## A Mighty Revelation

"Of the interlocking political systems that are the foundation of our nation's politics, the one that we all learn the most about growing up is the system of patriarchy, even if we never know the word, because patriarchal gender roles are assigned to us as children and we are given continual guidance about the ways we can best fulfill these roles." —bell hooks, Essay: "Understanding Patriarchy"

My studies at Princeton Theological Seminary initiated my search for a god who looks like me. In a lecture about "inclusive language," the professor reminded us that our earliest Sunday School lessons taught us that god was a spirit and could not be contained within any one image. That even though the male pronoun was used, all images were actually metaphors, pointing toward that which could not be fully known or named. He suggested that we experiment with alternate names and images of the divine and listed a few, including "Mother God." His suggestion launched my journey toward the feminine face of the divine.

On that day I realized that I had not been told the truth in my male-centered religious past. The literal male god they demanded that we obey turned out to be a metaphor around which a male-centered set of stories and myths had been written. I became suspicious of everything I was taught in religion's name and outraged that male-centered catechisms, dogmas, myths, and teachings had shaped my self-understanding, my relationship to men (who look like the male god), and my vocational options.

Fueled by my outrage, I wrestled with the names and images of god, the stories and myths of traditional religion, and the concepts of sin, savior, and salvation that pursued me into adulthood. Throughout these explorations, I caught glimpses of an unknown story that shadowed the formation of the Hebrew Scriptures and Christian Bible. There was a time when the divine looked like me.

### The Mother Goddess

I wondered how the writers and editors of religion's sacred books had been able to obscure the feminine face of the divine so completely that there was no a trace of her in my religious training except in the outrage of the prophets directed at false gods and pagan idols. In my search for the whole truth, I explored the historical and archaeological evidence supporting the fact that the most ancient image of the divine was female, and that this image reached back at least 25,000 years, long before god the father was imagined into being.

The Goddess has been called by many names. In the prophet Jeremiah's time, she was worshipped as the "Queen of Heaven." Her followers offered her "cakes," thought to have been in the shape of a woman's body. Jehovah's words to Jeremiah, however, convinced me as an adolescent that there was only one true god and that there would be grave consequences if I worshipped false gods like the Queen of Heaven:

> "Do you not see what is going on in the cities of Judah and the streets of Jerusalem? Children gather wood, the fathers kindle the fire, and the women knead the dough to make cakes in honor of the queen of heaven; and drink-offerings are poured out to other gods than me, all to provoke and anger me."

I discovered that biblical translators and scholars made translation choices that further obscured the divine feminine in religion's sacred texts. "El Shaddai," for example, is a name used for god in the Hebrew Scriptures. One of the original meanings of "shaddai" is "breast." The translators chose to use its alternate meaning, "high places." Thus, what might have been an affirming image for those of us with a female body was ignored in order to maintain the idolatry of the male god—the translators chose "God of the High Places."

Tragically, the worship of the Goddess was systematically annihilated by monotheism's armies. Her temples were destroyed. Her writings were burned. Her symbols were co-opted. Her followers were raped, persecuted, and murdered. I was horrified that all the while I was taught to worship the one true male god and to have no other gods before him, many of the "false gods" referred to in the Old Testament were Goddesses who looked like me. As an adolescent, I had applauded the zeal of the prophets in ferreting out false gods. Thus, I had been drafted into patriarchy's cheerleading squad to celebrate the annihilation of a god who looked like me.

As I awakened from patriarchy's stupor, I read and reread the Biblical stories of women and the pivotal myths of humankind's beginnings found there. I realized that Eve's story had been twisted out of shape to fit into the patriarchal narrative that woman came from man—thus the reversal of biological process in Genesis. And that woman catapulted humankind into sin—thus Eve's forbidden bite into the apple. These alterations were intentional and shaped the misogynistic rationalizations of the early church "fathers" and the architects of Western civilization. A demoted Eve became the queen-pin of patriarchy's assault on womankind.

Each revelation was almost too much to bear. I was livid and wanted to leave the church. In response the women whispered across the centuries in the fragments of their forgotten stories:

> Do not leave until you tell our stories, for in the telling you will hear your own stories, and those of your mothers and grandmothers.

Do not leave until you free us from men's interpretations.

    Our stories reach back in time before we were imprisoned within Hebrew

    and Christian myths. In our freedom, you will discover your own.

Do not leave until you recover our former glory.

    Free our voices to shout out the pain and courage of a lifetime.

    As it was in the *very* beginning, may it be now.

I kept my promise to the women of old by writing the book *A God Who Looks Like Me: Discovering a Woman-Affirming Spirituality* in 1995. And now, I am completing this book—*Eve, Our Mythic Mother*—to fulfill more of my promise and to include a respectful bow to Lilith and Mary whose stories intersect with Eve's at crucial points in the development of religion's misogynistic reworkings of ancient history.

Eve, Lilith, and Mary became my Mythic Mothers. As I uncovered their stories from the very beginning, they evolved into a powerful Trinity of inspiration, empowerment, and self-love. As I encountered the Goddess in them, I realized that nothing was wrong with me as Eve's daughter. As I descended into the depths of my own life, I discovered that SHE had been there all the time. Her presence restored me to a loving relationship with myself.

## Re-Socialization

Eve, Lilith, and Mary, extricated from the patriarchal narrative, re-socialized me and altered the trajectory of my life. Re-socialization is an essential task for those of us who desire to be free of the patriarchal constraints and the distorted self-understandings we inherited. It takes time and intentionality to exorcise the patriarchal narrative from within us. That narrative shaped the development of our thoughts, emotions, self-understanding, relationships, and career choices. In Gerda Lerner's words:

> "To step outside of patriarchal thought means: Being skeptical toward every known system of thought; being critical of all assumptions, ordering values and definitions. Being critical toward our own thought, which is, after all, thought trained in the patriarchal tradition. Finally, it means developing intellectual courage, the courage to stand alone, to reach farther than our grasp, to risk failure." —*The Creation of Patriarchy*

During my elementary school years at St. Joseph's Village, a home for dependent children, the content of my self-understanding, the extent of my vocational options, and the list of female qualities I was to emulate were shaped by the Catholic nuns. They lived beneath the shadow of "God the Father," in service to the male priests and to a male-centered understanding of the world and their place in it. As a result, we were taught that girls must stay in their place as secondary to and supportive of the male. And because we did not bear a physical resemblance to god, we could not be priests or altar boys.

> "Women simply cannot symbolize Jesus in his role as bridegroom of the Church, in his marital sacrifice for his bride the church. Women cannot symbolize Jesus *as a husband*, so they cannot symbolize Jesus at Mass." —JP Nunez, *The Catholic Exchange*

The nuns gave me *The Manual of Catholic Devotions,* which I read daily. As I walked through my personal history, it became clear that the Manual, along with daily Mass and weekly "confession" to the priest were the primary tools of indoctrination used at St. Joseph's. The Mass was a daily reminder that the boys looked like god and Jesus, and I didn't. Regular confession of my sins to the priest reminded me that I was a sinner and in need of weekly absolution. And preparing for confession birthed an exhausting hypervigilance about my words and actions. The focus on sin gave shape to the question "what did I do wrong," which eventually became the even more pernicious question "what's wrong with me."

During my high school and college years, I was immersed within the male-dominant teachings of Protestant fundamentalism. The boys in our youth group were groomed to be ministers, leaders, and world-changers. We, the girls, no matter how gifted, were groomed to be ministers' wives. We were encouraged to cultivate a set of capacities, including self-sacrifice and self-denial, that would eventually support our husband's "higher" calling.

> "Women should be excluded from pastoral leadership because man was first in creation and woman was first in the Edenic fall. We encourage women's service in all aspects of church life other than pastoral functions and leadership roles that entail ordination."
> —Southern Baptist Church: "Ordination and Role of Women in Ministry"

In my thirties I walked away from religion. Gerda Lerner and Elizabeth Cady Stanton played a major role in my re-socialization. Elizabeth Cady Stanton's 1892 essay-turned-book *The Solitude of Self* became my guidebook. Deeply transformed by her words, I sought out opportunities to develop self-sovereignty, which inspired the book *I Promise Myself: Making a Commitment to Yourself and Your Dreams*. She also challenged me to develop self-reliance, which inspired the book *Be Full of Yourself: The Journey from Self-Criticism to Self- Celebration*. In her own words:

> "The strongest reason why we ask for woman a voice in the government under which she lives; in the religion she is asked to believe; equality in social life, where she is the chief factor; a place in the trades and professions, where she may earn her bread, is because of her birthright to self-sovereignty; because, as an individual, she must rely on herself."

In addition, every word in Gerda Lerner's book *The Creation of Patriarchy* became my north star. Deeply challenged by her words, I sought out opportunities to develop intellectual arrogance, which led to my first book *A God Who Looks Like Me*, and supreme hubris, which inspired me to reject the male-centered.precepts of traditional recovery programs and replace them with woman-affirming alternatives in the book *A Deeper Wisdom*.

> "Perhaps the greatest challenge to thinking women is the challenge to move from the desire for safety and approval to the most 'unfeminine' quality of all, that of intellectual arrogance, the supreme hubris which asserts to itself the right to reorder the world." —Gerda Lerner

Reclaiming the stories of Eve, Lilith, and Mary introduced me to the truth, and it was that truth that re-configured my life, expectations, and self-understanding. The truth introduced me to a radically expanded set of qualities to nurture within myself and within circles of women, qualities which we will explore throughout this book. As we exorcise the men in our heads and replace them with the truth of a woman's life, we reclaim our "birthright to self-sovereignty" and nurture that birthright in our daughters.

## Called to Serve

I experienced my first call to be in service to the human community while at St. Joseph's Village, inspired by the nuns whose lives were committed to service. This calling was reinforced during my years in a non-denominational Protestant church. Calvary Gospel Church (CGC) supported my newly sober, single-mother to retrieve me from St. Joseph's. The new church encouraged all of us in the youth group to attend a Christian college, which we did. Upon graduation from college, I accepted the position of Religious Education Director at CGC.

Years later, one of my male friends from our high school youth group was "called" to be the minister of this same church. He looked like god—I didn't. Clearly, official ministry, as priest or minister, was off-limits to me. It was at Princeton Seminary that I discovered more progressive versions of Christianity that welcomed women into ordained ministry. By that time in my life, however, I no longer believed in a male god and had no desire to serve "him" in ministry.

I was introduced to Humanism in the 1990s. I am one among millions in the US and billions around the world who are religiously-unaffiliated. We are the ones who check "none of the above" when asked to identify our religion on various surveys. Demographers have given us the name "NONES." We are considered "non-believers" because most of us do not believe in a god nor do we subscribe to supernatural beliefs. Consequently, we do not submit to religion's dogmas and mandates. We are the fastest growing demographic in the United States.

Within the "secular" category, I identify myself as a non-theistic Humanist. My Humanist beliefs were shaped by natural rather than supernatural sources and by a focus on life here and now rather than on an afterlife. I call upon the resources held within my beliefs in times of confusion, challenge, and celebration. Having finally discovered a community within which I experience the deepest breath and widest embrace, I chose to be endorsed as a Humanist Chaplain.

***So, you ask, how does the Goddess fit into my non-theist perspective?***

First of all, the study of pre-patriarchal history and the primacy of the Goddess is an essential and deeply empowering task for those of us who grew up feeling other than the male god of traditional religion. Retrieving the stories of Eve, Lilith, and Mary from the patriarchal vortex is necessary to exorcise the internalized misogyny that trickles down to all of us, shaping our understanding of ourselves and our place in the larger scheme of things.

Secondly, my religious journey, exposing the lies I was taught in the church and choosing Humanism as my guiding light, doesn't mean that I live an imagination-free life. Preparing for breast surgery, I conjured up a "Goddess with Breasts Like Mine," born of my imagination and visions of early goddesses. She was not a power outside of me, but an imaginative support from the depth of my resilience.

Thirdly, my intellectual journey, dismantling patriarchy's infrastructure within me, has equipped me to accompany women as they sort through the remnants of their religious pasts. These remnants pursue us into adulthood and interfere with the development of a self-defined spirituality. The sorting process frees our imagination from the crippling effects of male-centered childhood myths and awakens our courage as we name our own gods and design our own woman-affirming spirituality. This sorting process also involves a reclamation of women's history, reaching back to the *very* beginning.

And finally, I am convinced that our deepest injuries are healed by a god who looks like us— even if we only glimpse her in one brief moment of freedom. Even if in the next moment, we move beyond gender in our understanding of the divine. Even if we eventually name ourselves atheist, humanist, or naturalist. Our empowerment deepens when the face of the divine reflects our own; when we imagine the divine in our image and likeness. And our empowerment is strengthened as we expand our awareness of women's history to include a time when the Goddess was honored as the Great Mother.

## Authenticity

Those who taught me in the churches of my early years believed that the Bible was the historically accurate literal word of god. There have been ongoing battles over the Bible's historical authenticity, but its authenticity really doesn't matter. It wouldn't matter if tomorrow the old and new testaments were categorically debunked as historical frauds, because I inhaled their "word of god-ness" based on the church's literal belief in and presentation of the stories, characters, and dictates found in that influential book. "Thus saith the Lord" takes up residence in our minds, hearts, and lives until his words are replaced by woman-affirming truths.

Transcending our early indoctrination does not happen by way of theological arguments or intellectual discussions. We cannot explore our religious past or design an updated belief system apart from our stories. Even the most abstract interpretations of religion are rooted in the life experience of those doing the interpreting. Since most of those writers and interpreters were men, their misogyny distorted the translations and interpretations we read. Therefore, it is women's stories that challenge and redefine religion from a woman's perspective.

As a result, my story is woven into the text of this book, including the religious universe within which I lived and the religious words and images that dominated my life from birth to 30. I was immersed within the genocidal commands of Jehovah, the Latin mass, the Virgin Mary, the sinful Eve, the absent Lilith, countless 'thus saith the lords,' and the patriarchally-inspired socialization I received as a girl-child. That is why this book's explorations are focused on Catholic and Protestant indoctrination, which include the Christian version of the Old Testament. This is what I know, what I can authentically write about, because I lived it.

If you are tempted to disregard this book's explorations because you "didn't have such an intense experience of religion;" or your "family was only nominally religious;" or you "left all that religious stuff behind;" read beneath the specific details and reflect on the ways patriarchy's delivery system of religious words, images, and expectations influences your life and family today. Perhaps one of the chapters will illuminate the origin of disturbing religious images and expressions that float through your mind and heart without your consent, making no sense given your non-religious past. Perhaps you will come to understand why the task of dismantling the idolatry of god the father in all its patriarchal, theocratic, white supremacist glory is the most significant challenge facing us in the 21st century.

Reading women's responses to my earlier books, I discovered that I was not alone as they shared their religious experiences with me. All of us were indoctrinated by the church or socialized by the patriarchal organization of our wider world, which trickled down to us in our families. All of us have been disempowered by the patriarchal infrastructure within which we live, whether delivered to us by the church and its holy books and rituals or by the family and its inherited customs and gender-specific treatment of its daughters and sons. We all must walk through this past in order to heal into the present.

## Breast—A Noun

To know anything at all
about our history,
our bodies, ourselves,
we must reach beyond
what they told us,
what they taught us,
what they want from us,
we must reach back
to the very beginning.

Before merriam and webster,
who have something to say
about everything: "breast a noun,
either of two milk-producing
glandular organs on the front of the chest
especially in the human female."

Before the reversals of christian history:
adam giving birth to the woman,
father god suckling the child,
christ nursing humanity,
the milk-giving goddess agatha
claimed as their saint, her breasts cut off
and carried on a platter.

Before the alterations of the hebrew bible:
el shaddai, a name for god,
shaddai meaning breast,
male translators altered the meaning,
their "god of the high places"
doesn't have breasts like mine.

We must reach back to the very beginning
to the place where lovers go
when they suck my breasts
to the source of life/mama mama mama
cried in the silence as their
wet lips surround my nipple
and they suck for dear life.

In the very beginning
long before adam gave birth
and father god sprouted breasts
and christ nursed humanity
and shaddai meant "high places"
and agatha's breasts were amputated
and my lovers wanted
more than I could give
in the very beginning was the big mama.

From her moon-breasts
flowed the milky way,
the stars and planets,
streams, rivers, and oceans,
all that ebbs and flows,
all that expands and contracts,
returning always to mama's breast.

To her breasts
pharaohs and kings
returned again and again hoping
to receive immortality
to become infants forever
nursing at mama's breast.

She came to me early in the morning
the one with breasts like mine
she held me in her arms
as i cried mama mama mama
don't let them take
my breast away on a platter
her nipple found my lips
and i sucked for my dear life.

The breast-less surgeon,
the one they call artist
he cut into my breast
with skill and beauty
and all they took away that day
was a perfectly shaped lump

they left the breast.

She came to me again that night
the one with breasts like mine.
She brought agatha
Agatha brought her platter

We made an altar
In the middle of the forest
on Agatha's platter we placed
using merriam and webster,
the hebrew scriptures,
the christian bible, and photos of lovers
who became infants at our breasts,
as kindling, we built a fire and
toasted marshmallows.

Where two or three women
are gathered together,
there SHE is in the midst of them.

Patricia Lynn Reilly

"It is thoroughly known that the only 'God image' ever painted on rock, carved in stone, or sculpted in clay, from the Upper Paleolithic to the Middle Neolithic —and that's roughly 30,000 years—was the image of a human female."
—Monica Sjoo and Barbara Mor, *The Great Cosmic Mother*

## A Pause Between Chapters to Clarify Terms
Misogyny, Sexism, Patriarchy, and Femicide

**Misogyny** defined as "the dislike of, contempt for, or ingrained prejudice against women, is expressed in many ways, including these:

1. At the level of speech and action, which is referred to as "**sexism**." Any act, speech, attitude, or theory which treats women as inferior to men is a form of sexism.

2. At the level of violence against women, including domestic violence, misogynistic terrorism, and "**femicide**," which is the intentional killing of women or girls because they are female.

3. At the level of over-arching institutional power, which is referred to as "**patriarchy**." Sexist practices become embedded within the patriarchal organization of a society.

"**Patriarchy** works on the principle that superiority justifies domination. What is common to all forms of patriarchy is male supremacy. In patriarchy, females are excluded from power and objectified, and males are born with a male gender privilege." —Pallavi Prasad, *The Difference Between Sexism and Misogyny, and Why It Matters*

"Women's scholarship has made it piercingly clear that **patriarchal naming of God** in the image and likeness of the powerful ruling man has the effect of legitimating male authority in social and political structures. In the name of the male Lord, King, Father God who rules over all, men have the duty to command and control: on earth as it is in heaven."—Elizabeth A. Johnson, *Naming God She: The Theological Implications*

"Like every means of social control, faith-based misogyny has its cost, and women have been made to pay an unequal fraction of the price." —Francine Prose, *"The Original Sin" in Lapham's Quarterly*

# CHAPTER 2

## The Genesis Mythology
### What's Wrong with Me?

*I do not permit a woman to be a teacher, nor must she domineer over man;*
*she should be quiet. For Adam was created first, and Eve afterwards; and*
*it was not Adam who was deceived; it was the woman who fell into sin.*
*—I Timothy 2:14, The New English Bible*

*"Throughout history, most of humankind's origin stories, hero's journey tales, novels, and*
*films have been created by men. Embedded in the stories are the values and priorities*
*we live by, and what we believe about women and men, power and war, sex and love."*
*—Elizabeth Lesser, Cassandra Speaks: When Women are the Storytellers*

During my years at seminary, I looked at my life through a wide-angle lens to consider the historical, religious, and familial contexts within which my attitudes toward myself had been shaped. On a societal level, I learned that male dominance was enshrined within our societal structure and that it had a name: patriarchy. I realized that I had been schooled and socialized within patriarchal Catholic and Protestant institutions for 30 years. I catalogued how this invisible social structure had shaped my life in those institutions and how its impact had trickled down to my mother and grandmothers' lives before me.

I came to understand that male violence is patriarchy's enforcer, and that the fear of rape and male violence is patriarchy's forceful reminder for us to stay in our place. I inventoried the specific consequences of that violence experienced in my family. My inventory included: observing daily domestic violence, spending 1 year in a children's shelter and 5 years in a Catholic orphanage, bouts of post-traumatic stress, horrific dreams, and an exhausting hypervigilance. One man held the power in our family and that power was supported by male ministers and priests who told my mother to return home to her violent husband and exhorted her to try harder to honor and obey him. As I acknowledged childhood's influence on my adult life, I chose to walk consciously through my past to heal into the present.

## What's Wrong with Me?

Simultaneously, I sought to unravel the "veil of shame," which was my constant companion since childhood. It was triggered in moments of visibility when I was receiving awards in grade school, performing in high school, excelling in college, lecturing after graduate school, handling callers' questions on talk radio, and facilitating creative book events for national tours. Words from my Catholic childhood and Protestant adolescence would rise up with a familiar refrain: who do you think you are; girls aren't supposed to be that confident; how dare you talk about god that way; you're committing blasphemy; you're too intense, too confident, too willful. In rare moments, the veil lifted, allowing me freedom of expression and a deep satisfaction with myself. I longed for those momentary feelings to be my ongoing experience.

When I entered into ministry among women, working in churches, hospitals, and women's shelters, and then eventually developing my own community ministry, I noticed that the self-critical question "what's wrong with me" found its way into every circle of women I facilitated, and that its pervasiveness cut across racial, ethnic, economic, religious, and generational boundaries. The question is evident in women's tendency to belittle themselves, to second-guess their impulses, to pathologize their decisions, and to theorize about their feelings. The question compels women to process every detail of their relationships and to attribute any positive achievement to an external force, ranging from a transcendent god, goddess, or higher power to a particular guru or self-improvement regimen. Unless there is an intervention, the question "what's wrong with me" accompanies us through every season of our lives.

The question "what's wrong with me" leads to the second question: "who will save me." Thus, our obsession is two-fold: finding out what's wrong with us, which then leads to a frantic search for the perfect savior, guru, teacher, procedure, or self-help regimen to save us, legitimize us, protect us, or transform us. There is no doubt in my mind that "what's wrong with me" and "who will save me" are the most devastating questions plaguing women's lives. The search for an answer and a savior of some sort consumes our valuable time, depletes our life energy, exhausts our limited resources. It distracts us from taking responsibility for our own lives and keeps us busy so that we don't have time to make a fuss, protest an injustice, or prepare our daughters for living in a world that prefers men.

> We frequent the therapist's office,
> > hoping the past holds an answer within it.
> We fill the churches,
> > maybe god knows the answer.
> We attend self-help meetings,
> > assured an answer is encoded within the Twelve Steps.
> We write "Dear Abbey" and every other expert,
> > certain that they must know the answer.
> We sit at the feet of spirituality gurus,
> > believing they will show us the way to an answer.

We buy every self-help book that hits the market,
        confident a new self-help project will quiet the question.
We consent to outrageous measures to guarantee our fertility
        or attract-ability, convinced that the presence of a child
        or a lover in our arms will dissolve the question.
We sign up for diet clubs and plans and spas,
        convinced our bodies are at the core of the answer,
        whatever it turns out to be.
We spend hundreds of dollars on new outfits to hide
        the question and on new body parts to eradicate the question.

And then at night after the day's search is over,
we binge on a quart of ice cream or a bottle of wine,
or we spend hours on the internet or cellphone
in tormented conversations trying to figure out
why the current relationship isn't working,
hoping that when we reach the bottom of the quart or bottle,
or the far reaches of the net or conversation,
things will have shifted deep within us
and once and for all we will know the answer
and what to do about it.

Yet no matter what we do in search of an answer:
no matter how much we lose or how slimming the dress,
no matter how expensive or authoritative the expert,
no matter how many babies, relationships, possessions we have or don't have,
no matter how spiritual, therapeutic, or recovered we become
we are left with the same question over and over again
as we look into the mirror horrified
that the restructuring of our relationship, our womb,
or our breasts did not quiet the question,
there it is in the morning, whispering from the mirror
"What's wrong with me? What's wrong with me?"
A mantra that accompanies us the length of our days.

*You are not alone in your search for an answer*
*to the question and a remedy to fix what's wrong with you.*
*Eve's daughters have been trying to get it right for centuries. (Patricia Lynn Reilly)*

## Religious Stories and Myths

In the course of completing this book, I was asked why I and other theologians do not leave the original biblical stories about our Mythic Mothers as they are, in all their messy, misogynistic, and murderous glory. In response, I told the questioner that ignoring the Bible's misogynistic stories would be like living in denial in a violent alcoholic home out of fear of the alcoholic's rage. Our denial and silence allow religion to continue to bring stress, fear, and violence to millions of girls and women around the world. And our denial and silence also allow religion to continue to shape the girl-child's experience of her own thoughts, feelings, body, and future. Most tragically, she is taught what it means to be a woman from those misogynistic stories.

We were also taught about our bodies and our responsibility to service men's needs in those stories. We were made aware of our secondary status in those stories. We were conditioned to help others and to swallow our anger in those stories. We were praised for our obedience and shunned for our trespasses based on those stories. Clearly, religious myths and stories hold within them tremendous power. Whether shouted at us from the pulpit or whispered to us in the culture, they exert a lasting influence on us.

Centuries ago, it was men who wrote down and then gathered together into sacred books the stories that were circulating by word of mouth throughout the Hebrew and early Christian communities. These storytellers, writers, and then translators were all rooted in a culture and society that worshipped god the father and thus preferred men. Their choice of what was meaningful and to be preserved, carried this dominant male perspective.

In both the Hebrew and Christian Scriptures, men's stories took center stage. In the unfolding process from telling to writing to translation, women's stories were lost or included only as they related to the more important stories of the men. In the process, women were dismissed and relegated to the margins of history and religion.

> • The Hebrew Scriptures are a record of the establishment of Israel as a nation and a religious community. The families within this community were male-dominated and their scripture supported the superiority of men in the home and community.

> • In the New Testament, we catch glimpses of the centrality of women in Jesus' ministry. After his death, however, the early Christian church adapted itself to the male-dominated structures of the surrounding culture by excluding women from leadership functions and relegating them to subordinate roles.

When we were growing up, the preachers and priests were men. Thus, the specific stories they chose to include in their teaching and preaching from the Christian Bible or the Hebrew Scriptures were influenced by that fact. As a result, we were not told the whole story in the formative years of our childhood and adolescence. The stories we did hear convinced us that women's stories were not as important as men's. And we learned the answer to the question "what's wrong with me" from those stories. According to the Genesis mythology, which we will explore in this chapter, and according to the pronouncements of the so-called "greatest minds of western civilization," which we will review in chapter 3, the answer to the question is that we are Eve's daughters and carry her sin and shame within our bodies and lives.

> "In my religious training, women were set aside and their worth centered around their passivity and submission. This contributed to my feelings of powerlessness and to the belief that my life is inconsequential." —Workshop Participant

> "I do not remember any stories about women in the church of my childhood. Religion was about men. The women were on the sidelines except for the Virgin Mary. The absence of women from religion mirrored my home. My mother was considered inferior. My father was the authority figure, and our lives revolved around him." —Workshop Participant

As the face of god changed in my experience, I searched for the stories of women in my religious past. It became apparent to me that healing into the present meant retrieving both our personal stories from their hiding places within the family memory, as well as the collective story of women from the margins of history and religion. To begin I gathered the fragments of women's stories from religious history by rereading the familiar Bible stories we heard over and over in our childhoods.

As I read these stories through the lens of my experience, strength, and hope as a woman, I became aware of the ways in which these stories had been distorted. I discovered that some of the familiar stories were read and studied only because of the importance of the man around whom the woman's story revolved. Women were given no voice in these stories. I also discovered that Eve, Lilith, and Mary's original stories were altered and their status reduced from Goddess to mouthpiece of patriarchy. Thus, they were imprisoned within men's mis-appropriation of their stories, status, and strength.

I discovered unfamiliar Bible stories that were seldom read in the churches and synagogues of our childhoods. These are graphic and brutal stories of violence against women. The stories of Tamar's rape by her brother Amnon (II Samuel) and of the gang rape and dismemberment of an unnamed concubine (Judges) were quickly passed over as the triumphant stories of their fathers, brothers, and male violators were read. And no one—either in the Biblical texts or from the pulpit expressed outrage at the treatment of the girls and women in these tragic stories.

I also became aware of unknown stories that were excluded from the Bible for a variety of reasons, depending on the particular viewpoint of the Rabbi or Church Father who gathered together the 'orthodox' stories. And yet, some of the excluded stories have been particularly stubborn and continue to survive on the margins of religious history. The story of Lilith is one of these stories being reclaimed by women today. (Chapter 6)

## A Motherless Beginning

As I shared in Chapter 1, I also heard rumors of a story that shadows the Bible and its development. There was a time when the divine looked like us. Tragically, the worship of Mother Goddess, was systematically destroyed. Her pre-genocidal story, however, reaches back before the Hebrew and Christian Scriptures were written. But in the churches of our childhood we were told, 'as it was in the beginning, it is now and ever shall be, world without end, amen'—and not surprisingly that beginning was defined by men. Throughout my exploration, however, I encountered woman-affirming stories from the *very* beginning.

Although intellectually the creation myths of Genesis may seem outdated and irrelevant, they continue to influence each of us. According to Genesis, the book of beginnings, there was no mother present at the creation of the world. The girl-child hears of a motherless beginning. It was the male god who brought the world into being through a series of verbal commands. The religion of my early years considered the creation myth of Genesis to be the literal truth. It would have been blasphemy to even suggest that the story was a myth woven from the imaginings of our Hebrew ancestors. Because of the literal nature of the teachings I received, the image of a male god ordering the world into being was firmly imprinted on my imagination. As Eve pointed out in the intro, most of us did not even notice the absence of the mother.

Whether the Genesis myth is considered a fanciful myth transmitted to us through the artwork, literature, and drama of our culture, or a literal description of creation pounded into us from the pulpit, the message of Genesis was clear: the god of the heavens was male and by the words of his mouth, the world came into being. The involvement of the mother as the source of life was effectively eradicated from the Genesis account of creation. It is necessary for us to acknowledge the absence of Mother from our beginnings. Her invisibility is one of the obstacles we face on our search for the truth of who we are.

Not only was the Mother absent during the creation of the world, the biological process of birthing was reversed so that it was out of man's rib that Eve was born. The tale of Adam, Eve, the rib, the apple, and the Fall is the most fully described Old Testament story in women's writings. We know this story. It was engraved on the canvasses, storybook pages, and memories of our childhoods. The information about Eve that women pick up in childhood is simple and very clear. In my workshops, each woman writes a story from childhood remembrances. This rendering of the story is typical:

Eve was Adam's wife. She was created from his rib. God told them not to eat the fruit of the special tree. The snake tricked Eve and she ate the apple. Then she seduced Adam and he ate it too. They were naked and put clothes on. Eve was bad, and because of her all women experience pain in process of giving birth.

It is apparent from women's writings that Eve's story defined the essence of womanhood, foretold the pain and suffering that would accompany a woman's life, and convinced us of our proper place in the scheme of thing. In circles of women, we explored the specific ways the traditional Eve story has affected women's lives, whether it was shouted at them as the literal truth in fundamentalism or subtly enforced within the family as they watched it imitated in their parents' lives and relationships. As you read the stories of workshop participants woven into the text below, *add your story to theirs.*

1. <u>Eve was Adam's wife. She was created from his rib.</u> The image imprinted on women's imagination is clear: A male god created Adam in his image. Eve was merely an afterthought. She was to keep the man company, to service him sexually, and to keep the garden neat and clean while Adam and god carried on the important business of running the world.

> "The story of Adam and Eve convinced me of the inferiority of women. Woman was given to man as property. This is how I defined 'a helper fit for him.' My sole purpose was to serve men. I was also convinced that Eve had a special connection with the devil. She brought death into the world."

> "The story of Adam and Eve was acted out on a daily basis at my house. I learned my role by watching my mom. My time, energy, and life were not my own. They were to be used in service of others. I was preparing to meet my own Adam and carry on the noble tradition."

2. <u>God told them not to eat the apple. The snake tricked Eve and she ate the apple. Then she seduced Adam and he ate it too. They were naked and put clothes on.</u>

> "Eve was morally weak and more susceptible to the wiles of the devil than the man was. She was the first to surrender to temptation. Her sexuality caused the downfall of humankind. I believed Eve was fatally flawed in some way that made her 'fall' inevitable. Her behavior proves the natural inferiority and fickleness of woman."

> "Eve was a manipulative temptress. She did something wrong. She symbolized a deep-seated corruption within women. Eve was so evil that she persuaded the most righteous man to sin. She used her sexuality as a weapon to seduce and destroy him. Her body and beauty tempted to men, and therefore were a negative influence."

3. <u>Eve was bad and God punished her.</u>

Pain and suffering are the lot of a woman's life. We continue to bear the brunt of Eve's act of defiance: we are to be submissive to men and we will experience pain and suffering in child-birth. Thus, Eve's shame and guilt are passed on to all women.

> "Every time I experienced pain in labor and delivery, I cursed Eve for her sin. On a primal level beyond any churchy kind of memories, I believed she was the cause of my pain. I was being punished because I was her daughter."

> "As a child I was sure Eve's sin had something to do with being curious. Women were curious and curious women got cast out of Paradise and turned into pillars of salt by angry male gods. They got sentenced to lives of pain and hard labor in the fields and in childbirth. It was all supposed to hurt because Eve was curious."

## Original Sin

*In iniquity I was brought to birth and my mother conceived me in sin. (Psalm 51:7)*

Clearly, religious language, imagery, and stories are powerful and exert a long-lasting influence on our lives. Through its words and stories, religion deposited shame and guilt within us. According to one interpretation of the Genesis story, god created the world in perfection. Then our original parents committed an act of disobedience instigated by Eve and paradise was lost. The children of Adam and Eve, you and I, are born with original sin. We are irrevocably flawed, without having taken any willful or conscious action, merely by reason of being born. No matter how hard we try to do what is right, we are sinful to our very core, and in need of a savior.

Although original sin is a shaming idea for all children, male and female, it carries an extra stigma for the girl-child, since we were taught that it was definitely Eve and not Adam who took the first bite of the forbidden apple. Eve shows up again and again in women's writings. She reminds us that we are responsible for humankind's sin. Leslie describes this awesome sense of responsibility: "As a girl-child, I felt responsible for anything negative that happened and for making whatever it was, right again."

The concept of original sin as hereditary sinfulness and the portrayal of Eve as the instigator of evil provided the cornerstone of my criticism-based childhood. It does matter what a community believes about its personal, historic, and mythic beginnings. The belief in original sin and the vilification of Eve trickled down and shaped the theological, educational, and developmental theory and practice that touched my body, mind, and spirit in childhood and adolescence. It affected the attitudes, behaviors, and disciplinary tactics used by surrogate parents, teachers, and religious care givers. It shaped their expectations of me and subjected me to a very different socialization regimen than the boys.

The emphasis on sin required constant vigilance as I scrutinized the minutest details of my every thought, motive, and action to expose the horrible monster, SIN. My growing personal concern about sinning crushed the free spiritedness of my early years. My natural spontaneity was replaced by a self-conscious monitoring of speech and action. My natural life-energy was depleted by an all-consuming observation of the self.

The early church fathers would have been proud of me, of us. We learned our lessons well. Tertullian was a powerful influence in the second century church. In his essay, *On the Apparel of Women,* he exhorts women with these words:

> "And do you not know that you are each an **EVE**. The sentence of God on this sex of yours lives in this age: the guilt must of necessity live too. You are the devil's gateway; the unsealer of that forbidden tree; the first deserter of divine law. You destroyed so easily God's image, On account of your desert— that is, death— even the son of God had to die."

Eve was exiled from the garden and shamed throughout religious history as a result of her 'sinful' deed. And from a tender age I, one of her daughters, was taught that whatever flowed naturally and spontaneously from within me was evil, wrong, and punishable. The question "what's wrong with me" punctuated my life as I searched far and wide for someone to give me an answer, for someone to offer me a magical insight, treatment, or cure. Most of us learned a shame-based way of perceiving ourselves and relating to the world. As a result, our natural tendency is to feel inadequate, that we're never quite good enough no matter what we do.

## Genocide: Re-writing Myths and Rousing Jehovah's Armies

Every culture has created stories to make sense of their beginnings. Although in one sense myths are narratives that lie outside of historical time, they are influenced by the values of the community within which they are invented. The values of the early male-dominated Hebrew community profoundly influenced the myths that were crafted to answer their questions about the origins of life. There is evidence, however, that the Genesis creation myths were not a benign attempt to answer the BIG questions, but rather, an intentional reversal of older female-oriented creation myths. A successful genocide requires an altered creation myth.

In the creation stories that trickle down to us from our earliest ancestors, the cosmos and its inhabitants, both human and divine, were birthed by the Great Mother. All gestated within Her body and emerged in the fullness of time. The Hebrew myth-makers rewrote these stories, in which the Mother had been very much present and active at the birthing of the world, into a creation 'out of nothing'. They replaced her with a male god who brought the world into being by a series of verbal commands. They transformed the snake, the Goddess' consort, into the devil, and the sacred grove in which the Goddess was worshipped into a forbidden place. These were intentional alterations, warning the Hebrew tribes not to engage in Goddess worship.

Not only was creation motherless, but when fragments of the feminine birthing imagery of these earlier myths found their way into the creation stories of Genesis, they were often altered to eliminate all connection to women. In ancient Mesopotamia, for example, it was believed that the Goddess made humankind out of clay and infused it with Her own menstrual blood, the fluid of life. In the verse, "Then the Lord God formed a man from the dust of the ground", we catch glimpses of this earlier time. Yet the misogynistic religious writers chose to translate ground as 'red clay' rather than its more accurate feminine interpretation, 'bloody clay'. In this inaccurate translation, lies a deep denial of woman and her involvement in the origins of life.

In the Assyrian Scriptures, the Goddess was referred to as "Mother Womb" and the "Creatress of Destiny." She created male and female in pairs. There are hints of this story in Genesis 1, but the writers changed 'she' to 'he'. "He" replaced the Goddess. This shift of pronouns indicates a shift of power and a rejection of the feminine.

| From the Assyrian Scriptures: | From Genesis 1: 27 |
|---|---|
| "The Mother-Womb, | "So God created man in his own image; |
| the Creatress of destiny, | in the image of God he created him; |
| In pairs she completed them. | male and female he created them." |

In Deuteronomy 32:18, Moses speaks these words to Israel: "You forsook the Rock that begot you and have forgotten the God that formed thee." The Hebrew word for 'begat' refers to the laboring action of a birthing woman, which is an exclusively female image. In certain translations, this verse is accurately translated. In others, the verse reads: "And (you) forgot the God who fathered you." This word choice is inaccurate and obscures the feminine qualities attributed to the Divine.

Moving beyond word alterations, I became aware of the treatment of the Goddess. She was considered a false god, an idol, and therefore, in competition with Jehovah whose armies rallied to destroy all remnants of Her and along the way, raped the youngest among her followers. She was referred to as "Asherah" in the Old Testament, and "asherim" were the symbols and objects used in Her worship.

- Deuteronomy 12: "You shall tear down their altars and smash their sacred pillars and burn their Asherim with fire, and you shall cut down the engraved images of their gods and obliterate their name from that place."
- 1 Kings 14: "The Lord will strike Israel, as a reed is shaken in the water; and He will uproot Israel from this land which He gave to the fathers, and He will scatter them beyond the River because they have made Asherim, provoking the Lord to anger."
- Numbers 31: "All the girls who have not known man intimately, spare for yourselves."

I also discovered verses chronicling the people's resistance to the prophet's threats of total destruction if they continued to worship the Goddess:

> Jeremiah 44:15-17: "[1]Then all the men who knew that their wives were burning incense to other gods, along with a large assembly of women who were present and all the people living in Egypt, said to Jeremiah, 'We will not listen to the message you have spoken to us in the name of the Lord. Instead, we will do everything we vowed we would do. We will sacrifice and pour out drink offerings to the goddess called the Queen of Heaven just as we and our ancestors, kings, and leaders previously did in the towns of Judah and streets of Jerusalem. For then we had plenty of food, were well-off, and had suffered no harm."

The genocide of the Goddess who reigned in peace for millennia, required a campaign of annihilation by Jehovah's armies (Chapters 1 and 2); a rewritten creation myth in which the male gives birth and the woman brings sin, suffering, and death into the world (Chapter 2) ; an intellectual rationale, asserting the inferiority of the female (Chapter 3); a fabricated biological doctrine, assigning men superiority (Chapter 3); and a reversal of value—the demotion of the Goddess and the violent ascendance of the male god (Chapter 4).

*Down became up, truth became lie.*
*Their twisted words became the 'Word of God.'*
*Our question becomes 'what's wrong with me.'*

### Suicide

The final recourse is suicide
successfully attempted
by many women throughout the ages.
The ultimate choice to transcend
the weakness
the responsibility
the harassment
of being female.

The way out of it all,
the final relinquishment,
to die in one dramatic moment
of courage and willfulness
or to slowly disappear
under layers of fat,
in a drug-induced stupor,
or in the vagueness
of an unformed life.

*Palladius traveled through Egypt in the fourth century to gather anecdotal tales of holy women and men. He recorded the story of Alexandra.*

A maidservant named Alexandra left the city and immured herself in a tomb. She received the necessities of life through a window, and for ten years never looked a woman or man in the face.

When asked why she lives in a tomb, she said, "A man was distracted in mind because of me, and rather than scandalize a soul made in the image of God, I betook myself to a tomb, lest I cause him suffering or reject him."

When asked how she perseveres, never seeing anyone, and battling against weariness, she said: "From early dawn to the ninth hour I pray while spinning flax. The rest of the time I go over in my mind the holy patriarchs, prophets, apostles, and martyrs. Then I wait patiently for my end with good hope."

Some women are murdered
by the words absorbed into their life-stream.
Like the steady drip of an IV inserted at birth
the words of the holy patriarchs, prophets,
apostles, and martyrs are responsible
for Alexandra's death.

Their words held her body responsible
for the distraction of men.
Their words slowly poisoned her
as they praised her virtue for successfully
surpassing the weakness of being female.
May she rest in peace.

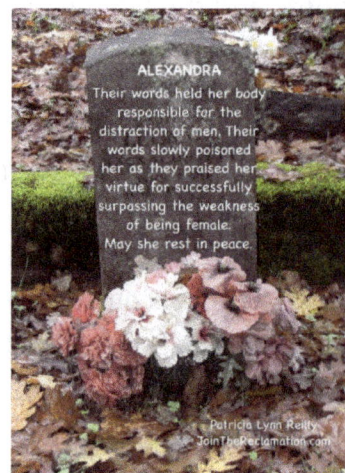

ALEXANDRA
Their words held her body responsible for the distraction of men. Their words slowly poisoned her as they praised her virtue for successfully surpassing the weakness of being female. May she rest in peace.

—Patricia Lynn Reilly
JoinTheReclamation.com

"At its most repugnant, the belief that women must be subjugated to the wishes of men excuses slavery, violence, forced prostitution, genital mutilation, and national laws that omit rape as a crime.

"But it also costs millions of girls and women control over their own bodies and lives, and continues to deny them fair access to education, health, employment, and influence within their own communities."
—Jimmy Carter, Speech to the Parliament of World Religions

# CHAPTER 3

---

## *A Symposium of Poisonous Words*
### On the Nature of Woman

*"The omission of women's history gives men the impression that they are much more important than they actually are. If a man thinks everything great in the world was created by men, then naturally he will look down on women. And naturally, we will have different aspirations for our sons than we do for our daughters."*
—Gerda Lerner, The Creation of Feminist Consciousness

Our free-thinking foremothers recognized that the rearrangement of society to allow women full political, social, and economic participation would not be sustainable unless women addressed their own internalized "oppression" and became willing to dismantle all remnants of it from their lives. They understood that centuries of "trickle down" had taken its toll on womankind as the ideas, theories, and theologies of influential men had become embedded within us. Lodged there, they monopolize our thoughts and actions, and our attitudes toward ourselves until we become willing to wrestle with them across a critical distance.

My first step was to unearth my college notes taken in various Western Civilization classes. This turned out to be an essential step in sorting through my religious past across a critical distance. At the time I wanted to identify my "internalized oppression," in order to break free of it. My first revelation was that I had inherited the question "what's wrong with me" from the architects of Western civilization, the so-called "greatest minds of Western thought." They were philosophers, theologians, historians, psychiatrists, and ministers—they were all male.

I was outraged at their self-serving dissection of the nature of women and the tenacious influence of their words, echoing across the centuries in male-centered philosophical, theological, and psychological theories and practices. Words, trickling down and touching our lives in the homes, churches, and schools of childhood. I traced the roots of my shame-based self-critical attitudes to three influential doctrines of Western civilization: the idolatry of the Judeo-Christian male god; the establishment of a hierarchical paradigm that assumes women's inferiority; and the historical linkage of women's inferiority with the veil of shame.

In this decade I turned toward their poisonous words once again, compelled by the blatant expressions of patriarchal privilege, male supremacy, and theocratic infrastructure-building happening all around us. I revisited the actual words of these men. Words, I took out the closet and placed within a fictional "Symposium on the Nature of Woman." My purpose this time was to identify how those very words are fueling the USA's current slide toward theocracy. Yes, the theocrats among us, including a majority of our current Supreme Court justices, consult these "greatest minds" to bolster their theocratic aspirations, including overturning Roe V. Wade.

I wanted to believe that their words were relics of a distant past, and then I remembered that in 2020, 47,000 women and girls worldwide were killed by their intimate partners or other family members; that our daughters continue to starve themselves and harm their bodies; and that our aging female friends continue to hide their brilliance because no one seems interested in listening to them now that they're OLD. And most recently, we were all confronted by their poisonous words held within the decisions handed down by the current Supreme Court. Clearly patriarchy is alive and well in 2022 and the old white male god still hovers above it all. Currently he is reasserting his dominance based on ancient myths and successful theocratic incursions.

## *The "Nature of Woman"*

I chose the topic for the Symposium after reading Freud's lecture, "On Femininity": *"Throughout history people have knocked their heads against the riddle of the nature of femininity. Nor will those of you who are men have escaped worrying over this problem; to those of you who are women this will not apply—you are yourselves the problem."*

Behind the words you will read here is an acknowledgement of the debt the architects of Western civilization believed they owed to the Hebrew tradition. Many of its stories, symbols, and mythologies were woven into the understandings of gender and morality that have defined cultural history throughout the ages. Their extended writings also celebrate the success of the Jewish patriarchs and the armies of monotheism who, in only six centuries, were able to successfully replace the worship of the Goddess with the worship of Yahweh/Jehovah. This success provided the architects of western civilization with two powerful notions, which served as the centerpiece of their self-serving investigations into the nature of woman's inferiority:

Notion 1—Life originated from the male, not the female.
Notion 2—The woman was the instigator of evil.

Representing diverse religious traditions and disagreeing heartily about many theological issues, I was astonished at the level of agreement among the Symposium speakers about the nature of women as supported by their self-serving definitions of natural law. In the words of Martin Luther, the Augustinian monk: "Clearly **EVE** is to blame. We can hardly speak of her without shame." Simply, as you will experience, the so-called "greatest minds of western civilization" were all in agreement—females are other than god, they are misbegotten males, and yes, there is something seriously wrong with them—they are the daughters of **EVE**. Inspired by Gerda Lerner, I claimed "intellectual arrogance" by actively engaging, and eventually exorcising, the poisonous words and ideas generated by the men who shaped the question "what's wrong with me" and provided the justification for my self-critical attitudes.

Below find excerpts from their writings. This is most certainly an excavation project to highlight the poison in their words while identifying the roots of our internalized oppression.

- Notice how **EVE** is scapegoated throughout the proceedings.
- Notice the qualities assigned to females and males based on their misogynistic worldview.
- Notice the emphasis on the inability of women to manage their own lives and bodies.
- Notice the responses of women who kept track of the words and phrases, childhood messages, and current experiences triggered as they engaged the men's poisonous words.
- Note that the final entry features Supreme Court Justice, Samuel Alito. His views were shaped by the writings of his misogynistic colleagues of an earlier era.

---

**ARISTOTLE of GREECE,** 384-323 B.C.E, was a student of Plato. He begins by setting forth his theory that all living things have souls, but that a woman's soul differs from a man's soul in three of its components: nutritive, sensitive, and rational. He then outlines the differences in the function, role, and place of men and women in the family and society:

"A woman's <u>nutritive soul</u> requires less nourishment than the man's. Her <u>sensitive soul</u> is devoid of sexual desire therefore she assumes the passive role in copulation. And her <u>rational soul</u> does not include the capacity to govern her own life and manage her own actions. Consequently, the husband, who is superior in reason, rules in the home. The wife is to obey. One of the functions of a village, as a conglomerate of households, is to supervise the activities of women. For nature has made the one sex stronger, the other weaker, that the latter through fear may be the more cautious, while the former by its courage is better able to ward off attacks, and that the one may acquire possessions outside the house, the other preserve those within."

Aristotle's Trickle-Down Effect: Women's Responses
- "A woman's place is in the home, safe and protected.
- "I can't leave my husband because I don't know how to manage without him."
- "I am embarrassed by my appetite. I need lots of food to maintain my energy. Sometimes I deny my body food based on the belief that women don't need as much as men."
- "My daughter read Aristotle in her philosophy class. She read a section aloud to me and said, 'This guy doesn't respect women.' I wondered what it means to her that one of the of the wisest men of the ages is misogynistic." (Mary Pipher)

---

**PHILO of ALEXANDRIA,** 20-50 C.E, Hellenistic Jewish philosopher, reads from his "Questions and Answers on Genesis, Book 1:"

Question: Why was not woman formed from earth instead of the side of the man?

Answer: "First because woman is not equal in honour with the man. Second, because she is not equal in age but younger. Wherefore those who take wives who have passed their prime are to be criticized for destroying the laws of nature. Third, he wishes that a man should take care of the woman as a necessary part of him; but the woman, in return should serve him as a whole. Fourth, he counsels man figuratively to take care of the woman as a daughter, and the woman is to honour the man as a father . . . "

Philo's Trickle-Down Effect: Women's Responses
- "My husband treats me like a child."
- "My dad said women are more gullible than men."
- "My boss talks down to me. He sounds like my father."
- "My father verbally battered my mother about her gray hair, extra weight, and wrinkles as she got older. In exchange for not leaving her for a younger woman, he demanded that she dress sexier and submit to his demeaning sexual antics."

---

**PAUL, THE APOSTLE**, 4 BCE-63 CE, represents the early Christian perspective and points out the practical ramifications of the sequence of creation and the disobedience of Eve.

I Timothy 2:9: "Let the woman learn in silence with all subjection. But I suffer not a woman to teach, not to usurp authority over the man, but to be in silence. For Adam was formed first, then EVE. And Adam was not deceived, but THE WOMAN being deceived was in transgression. Notwithstanding she will be saved in childbearing, if she continues in faith, and in charity and holiness with sobriety."

Paul's Trickle-Down Effect: Women's Responses
- "I get quiet around men."
- "I feel uncomfortable chairing meetings with men present as if I'm stepping outside acceptable bounds."
- "My parents made it very clear that they wouldn't come to my wedding if a woman officiated. In their view a female minister goes against the natural order of things."
- "My father made some stupid decisions that hurt our family while I was growing up. I asked my mother why she didn't intervene. She said that Dad only listened to men and that her feedback wasn't acceptable as women aren't as smart as men."

---

**TERTULLIAN,** CHURCH FATHER, 160-230 CE, reiterates how important it is that women's clothing and appearance reflect their status as **EVE**'s daughters. He reads from *On the Apparel of Women*:
No one of you, from the time she had first learned the truth concerning woman's condition, would have desired too gladsome a style of dress; so as rather to go about in humble garb, and rather to affect meanness of appearance, while walking about as an EVE, mourning and repentant in order that by every garb of penitence she might the more fully expiate that which she derives from **EVE**—the ignominy of the first sin, and the odium of human perdition."

"An Appeal to the Virgins: Veil your head: if a mother, for your sons' sakes; if a sister, for your brethren's sakes; if a daughter for your fathers' sakes. All ages are periled in your person. Put on the panoply of modesty; surround yourself with the stockard of bashfulness; rear a rampart for your sex, which must neither allow your eyes egress or ingress to other people. Wear the full garb of women, to preserve the standing of virgin."

<u>Tertullian's Trickle-Down Effect: Women's Responses</u>
- "I always feel like I'm wearing a veil, covering aspects of myself so others won't be intimidated."
- "I feel responsible when men gawk at me when I walk down the street. They are the ones gawking and I'm the one feeling responsible."
- "My father is Islamophobic except when it comes to the veiling of women. He thinks all women should be veiled to signify their inferiority to men."
- "I feel weird about my body and go through daily conflict over what to wear. I can't wear anything tight because then I have to deal with men sexualizing me."

**AUGUSTINE**, 354-430, is the African Bishop whose writings emphasized the hierarchic principle laid out in Genesis: "We do not possess equality of standing because each of us is subordinated to the one above. Based on the sequence of creation, the headship and dominion of men are divinely ordained. EVE was created because the man needed a helpmate."

From *The Literal Meaning of Genesis:* "I don't see what sort of help woman was created to provide man with, if one excludes procreation. If woman is not given to man for help in bearing children, for what help could she be? To till the earth together? If help were needed for that, man would have been a better help for man. The same goes for comfort in solitude. How much more pleasure is it for life and conversation when two friends live together than when a man and a woman cohabitate?"

<u>Augustine's Trickle-Down Effect: Women's Responses</u>
- "Mom resents that my dad's most meaningful conversations are with his male friends."
- "The men in my family continue to believe that their girlfriends and wives are their god-given helpmates. Women are expected to handle everything from cooking the meals to doing the laundry to meeting the male's sexual needs, anytime, anywhere."

**THOMAS AQUINAS**, 1225-1274, is the Dominican Friar who participated in the ecclesiastical councils that developed Catholic theology. He reads from *Summa Theologica*:

"As regards the individual nature, woman is defective and misbegotten, for the active force in the male seed tends to the production of a perfect likeness in the masculine sex; while the production of the female comes from defect in the active force or from material indisposition or even from some external influence."

"Subjection is two-fold. One is servile, by which the superior makes use of a subject for his own benefit; and this kind of subjection came after sin. By economic or civil subjection, the superior makes use of his subjects for their own benefit and good. And this kind of subjection existed before sin. For good order would have been wanting in the human family if some were not governed by others wiser than themselves. So, woman is by nature subject to man, because in man the discretion of reason predominates."

### Aquinas' Trickle-Down Effect: Women's Responses

- "I was taught that feelings were less important than thoughts. And because boys think and girls feel, girls are less important than boys."
- "Women were not trusted in our family because their feelings kept them from getting the job done. They were fickle. Men were in charge because they had no feelings and finish the task at hand. They were rational."
- "I overheard the guys at work say that women are too emotional and good for nothing especially 'at that time of the month.' Men could be counted on all the time."

---

**MARTIN LUTHER**, 1483-1546, is the Augustinian Friar who founded Protestantism. Luther reads from "Woman Unexcelled if She Stays in Her Sphere:"

"Men are commanded to rule and reign over their wives and families. But if a woman forsaking her position, presumes to rule over her husband, she engages in a work for which she was not created, a work which stems from her own failing and is evil. For God did not create this sex to rule. For this reason, domination by women is never a happy one. The history of the Amazons, celebrated by Greek writers, might be advanced against this view. But I believe what is told of them to be a fable."

### Luther's Trickle-Down Effect: Women's Responses

- "When I speak my mind in my marriage, there's conflict. My mother says I'm going against natural law when I'm not submissive."
- "On my wedding night my mother told me not to refuse my husband's sexual advances. She believes it's a woman's duty to meet her husband's needs no matter how uncomfortable or painful the experience."

---

**HEINRICH KRAMER AND JAMES SPRENGER** were the Dominican monks appointed by Pope Innocent VIII in 1484 to ferret out the heresy of witchcraft. They authored a handbook, outlining the official methodology for persecuting witches. They launched the church's successful attack on Mother Goddess worship and its successful restriction of women's power in the church and society. They read from their influential treatise: "The Malleus Maleficarum:"

"Since women are feebler both in mind and body, it is not surprising that they should come under the spell of witchcraft. For as regards intellect or the understanding of spiritual things, they seem to be of a different nature from men. But the natural reason is that she is more carnal than man, made clear by her many carnal abominations. There was a defect in the formation of THE FIRST WOMAN since she was formed from a bent rib of the breast, bent in a contrary direction to a man. Since through this defect SHE is an imperfect animal, SHE always deceives."

### Kramer/Sprenger's Trickle-Down Effect: Women Respond

- "I was taught to fear witches and to remember how they ended up. My secret fascination with their power frightened me."
- "Independent women were always put down in my family. We were warned against being strong and independent through jokes, sarcasm, and innuendo."

---

**JEAN-JACQUE ROUSSEAU**, 1712-1778, believed that educational systems should encourage the development of only those qualities which guarantee "right order and patrilineal inheritance." Given that chastity was considered the quintessential female virtue, he recommended that the sexual energies of young girls be repressed to encourage chastity and that the autonomous energies of girls be redirected into obedience and fidelity in service to the man.

### From "Emile"

- "In the union of the sexes . . . it is necessary the one should have both the power and the will, and that the other should make little resistance. The principle being here established, it follows, that woman is expressly formed to please man."
- "Woman and man were made for each other; but their mutual dependence is not the same. The man depends on the woman, only on account of their desires; the woman on the man, both on account of their desires and their necessities. We could subsist better without them than they without us. Their very subsistence and rank in life depend upon us, as does our estimation of their charms and their merit."
- "By the law of nature itself, both women and children lie at the mercy of men; it is not enough they should be beautiful, it is requisite their charms should please. Their glory lies not only in their conduct, but in their reputation; and it is impossible for women who consent to be infamous, to be ever virtuous."

### Rousseau's Trickle-Down Effect: Women's Responses

- "My partner seems less attached to us than we are to him. In many ways we are not as necessary to him as he is to us."
- "I was afraid of being called a whore even though I didn't know what that word meant. If we stepped outside of the lines, we were marked for life."
- "I was taught that a girl's reputation was her most valuable asset. If I squandered it by exploring my sexuality, I became damaged goods and undesirable to men."

---

SIGMUND FREUD, 1856-1939, was an Austrian neurologist and the founder of psychoanalysis. He clarifies the nature of the clitoris in his treatise titled Femininity:

"The castration complex of little girls is started by the sight of the genitals of the other sex. They notice the difference and, it must be admitted, its significance too. They feel seriously wronged, often declare that they want "to have something like it too," and fall victim to "envy for the penis," which will leave ineradicable traces on their development and the formation of their character, and which will not be surmounted in even the most favorable cases without a severe expenditure of psychical energy.

"The wish to get the penis in spite of everything may contribute to the motives that drive a mature woman to analysis, and what she may reasonably expect from analysis—a capacity, for instance, to carry on an intellectual profession—may often be recognized as a sublimated modification of this repressed wish."

Freud's Trickle-Down Effect: Women's Responses
- "Any woman who pursued a career was called a "dyke" by my father, meaning a masculinized and unacceptable woman."
- "I was told that if I masturbated, I would ruin my chances for a good sexual relationship with a man by using up my limited sexual energy on myself."
- "I feel ashamed because my husband knows my body better than I do."

---

KARL BARTH, 1886-1968, the 20th-century theologian reads from his book Church Dogmatics: "The Ordering of Male and Female."

"Man and woman stand in sequence. Man has his allotted place and the woman hers. Man and woman are not an A and a second A whose being and relationship can be described like the two halves of an hour glass, which are obviously two, but absolutely equal and therefore interchangeable. Man and woman are an A and a B, and cannot, therefore be equated. A precedes B, and B follows A. Order means succession. It means preceding and following. It means super- and sub-ordination. Properly speaking, the business of woman, her task and function, is to actualize the fellowship in which man can only precede her, stimulating, leading and inspiring."

Barth's Trickle-Down Effect: Women's Responses
- "I've been looking for an "A" all my life. What is the purpose of a "B" without an "A" to precede it? Barth's words gave voice to my life-long quest."
- "The men in my life have always been taller, smarter, and wealthier than I am. The only possible relationship is one in which the man is dominant and I am subordinate."
- "Men's interests and careers are much more important than mine. I've expanded my life to include their interests and set aside jobs to support their careers. They've never shown any interest in anything of importance to me."

---

**SAMUEL ALITO** is the Supreme Court Justice who wrote the 2022 draft opinion overturning Roe v. Wade. He is an originalist who believes the Constitution should be interpreted as it would have been understood by the Founders when they wrote it. Tragically for women, the founders were misogynists who believed women were the property of men and therefore, women's lives, bodies, and processes were to be managed by men.

> "At least seven times, Alito cited Sir Matthew Hale, a 17th-century jurist who didn't think marital rape was possible because wives were the property of their husbands, and who sentenced at least two women to die for witchcraft. Alito also cited a legal text from 1250 by Henry de Bracton that says women are inferior to men, and that they sometimes give birth to literal monsters." —Gillian Brockell, The Washington Post: "Abortion in the Founders' Era: Violent, Chaotic, and Unregulated"

> "Alito relies on sources such as Hale without acknowledging their entanglement with legalized male supremacy. The men who cited Hale as they constructed the early American legal order refused to give women the right to vote or to otherwise enjoy full citizenship. Relying on that history of injustice as a reason to deny modern women control over their own lives is a terrible argument . . ." —Jill Elaine Hasday, Washington Post: "On Roe, Alito Cites a Judge who Treated Women as Witches and Property"

---

## A Deep Breath

I invite women to eavesdrop on the symposium and grapple with the ideas of these influential men just as free-thinking women have done throughout history. As they engage the symposium with their minds, bodies, and hearts, with all of their intelligences, they have a variety of reactions. Some women believe they are incapable of grappling with ideas. In the presence of men and their ideas, these women feel intimidated and assume a one-down position. At a loss for how to meaningfully participate, they become quiet and dissolve into a familiar invisibility. One participant wrote, *"Without the support of women, I could not have engaged the words of the symposium participants. Like god, they have always seemed untouchable and to disagree with them would be irreverent and arrogant. They are the first men whose ideas I've taken on."*

Women were taught not to question the ideas and opinions of the "fathers." As we critically distance from their ideas and consider this material together, it isn't unusual for women to have dreams of our meeting space being vandalized, of god the father ranting and raving from the heavens, and of witch-burnings and heresy trials. In addition, women are afraid of the intensity of feeling that may surface once their eyes are opened to the wider reality of a woman's life. A woman's intensity makes everyone uncomfortable, including herself. We were taught to be nice, not angry even when our lives and sanity are at stake.

To explore our communal past touches a deep rage within us—the accumulated rage of generations of women who believed the lies they were told about themselves and then passed those lies on to their daughters and granddaughters. One workshop participant wrote: *"Rage moves through my body. I am in shock that the fathers of history wrote this stuff and that we were exposed to their writings. Their notions are so insidious and damaging. The symposium feels like a necessary wake-up call."*

### Historical Trickle-Down

As I imagined the good old boys hanging around after the symposium, patting each other on the back, networking across the centuries, applauding their successful dissection of the nature of woman, and celebrating their impressive unanimity, I realized all that I had absorbed their words like the steady drip of an IV inserted at birth. Their words trickling down to me by way of history lessons in elementary and high school; philosophy and theology lectures in college and graduate school; countless homilies in the Catholic church and sermons in the Protestant church; daily Bible readings; advertisements and television programs; and societal expectations, family customs, and parental mantras.

Trickle-Down 1: The words written by the "architects of western civilization" were based on men's experience, and celebrated men's superiority in thought, body, value and achievement. Clearly, it has been men, limited by their psycho-social projections; their sexual anxiety, discomfort, and insecurity; and their ignorance and dismissal of the female experience who have shaped the intellectual, philosophical, theological, and mythic traditions passed on to us. All claims to objectivity dissolve. These men were writing from their perspective as men, subject to the distortions inherent within a male-centered worldview.

---

Trickle-Down 2: The words written by the "architects of western civilization" set forth women's inferiority of thought, body, spirit, achievement, and value as an undisputed article of faith supported by natural and divine law. The fact that we are the daughters of EVE is the crux of our problem according to the myth-makers reviewed in Chapter 2 and the "greatest minds" reviewed in this chapter. EVE was given a pivotal role in men's developing mythology. The mythmakers' reversal of biological process established Adam as the first "A" and EVE as the first "B." This influential notion has legitimized our inferiority throughout the ages.

---

Trickle-Down 3: The words written by the "architects of western civilization" assumed that shame was an essential female characteristic. The historical linkage of women's constitutional inferiority with shame has been used to keep women in line for centuries. Throughout the development of Western civilization, women were expected to wear shame like a garment, a covering, and a veil to remind them of their inferiority and their proper place in the hierarchic scheme of things, and to protect others from the peril and temptation of their unveiled presence. Thus, the veils and "habits" worn by the nuns who cared for me as a child.

Shame was also to be demonstrated in a woman's behavior: a virtuous woman was silent, shy, chaste, obedient, discreet, restrained, timid, and passive. A virtuous woman lowered her head and her eyes to avoid direct eye contact with men, blushed to acknowledge the embarrassment of being female, covered her head to indicate her subordination to her husband's authority, and covered her body to protect men from the peril of her natural seductiveness.

Shame was to be illustrated in the amount of space a woman occupied. A virtuous woman made herself small to fit into the scheme of things. Her feelings remained quiet and acceptable; her thoughts, tame and unthreatening; her needs, silent and non-existent; her appetites, manageable. A virtuous woman took up very little space with her body. She was and still is in danger of disappearing.

On the other hand, shameless women refused to stay in line. As a result, they were condemned for their audacity to refuse "B" status and their arrogance to step into "A" status beside men. They continue to be damned for exhibiting the unbecoming qualities of immodesty and personal ambition, and for upsetting the divine order of things. In second-century Rome an unfaithful wife's humiliation was made into a public spectacle. She was paraded nude on a donkey into the town center, vulnerable to the crowd's insults and mockery. A sexually autonomous woman was without shame and was not to be tolerated.

## Outside The Symposium: Women's Voices

There have always been women
who remember the old ways.
Women who hold within them
the memory of a time
in the very beginning
when women were honored.
Women who refuse
to worship the gods,
to learn the language,
to take the names
of the fathers.

Women who refuse to twist
their female bodies out of shape

to fit into definitions,
to transcend limitations.
Women who love their bodies.
Regardless.

Women who refuse to please others
by becoming smaller than they are.
Women who take space
with their thoughts and feelings,
their needs and desires,
their anger and their dreams.

I imagine them outside the symposium
loud and strong women from every age
wild women   spinster women
wise women   rebellious women
women who love women
midwives. witches   healers   activists.
Banners and placards aloft . . .

> Eve, the Mother of All Living
>> Take and eat of the good fruit of life. Take a big bite!

> Sappho
>> She Who Gives Birth Has Power over Life and Death

> Mary Wollstonecraft
>> Break the Silken Fetters

> Sojourner Truth
>> Ain't I a Woman?

> Margaret Sanger
>> "Speak and Act in Defiance of Convention"

> Karen Horney
>> "Womb Envy is More Like It"

> Elizabeth Cady Stanton
>> "Whatever the Bible may be made to do in Hebrew and Greek
>> in plain English it does not exalt and dignify women."

> bell hooks
>> "I will not have my life narrowed down. I will not bow down to
>> somebody else's whim or to someone else's ignorance."

Audre Lorde
"The Master's tools will never dismantle the master's house."

Women's speeches and songs
questions and answers
suspicion and anger
greeting the men
as they emerge from the symposium.

One by one the women step up
and speak the truth of a woman's life
they commit the forbidden act
of biting into patriarchal thought
refuting it, smashing it,
discarding it and beginning again
in the very beginning when women
loved their bodies     named their gods
authored their lives
when women refused to surrender
except to life as it pulsated through them.

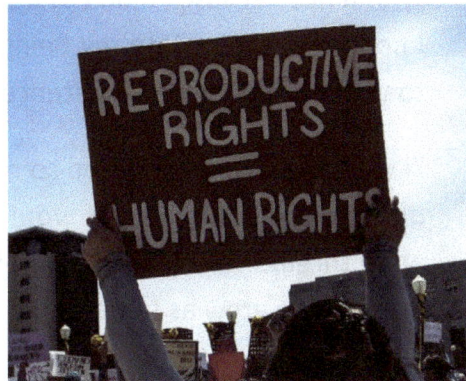

Women full of themselves
their ideas     their stories
their anger     their passion.
Women reminding us
there is nothing wrong
there never has been anything wrong
there never will be anything wrong with woman
that's why nothing ever works.
Stop asking the question!     (Patricia Lynn Reilly)


### Unacceptable Words: Evelyn's Story

"Working my way through the symposium brought up an old sense of being intimidated by ideas and concepts. I am an intelligent woman yet family and school experiences convinced me that something was wrong with me intellectually. It continues to be a challenge for me to let go of the old vision of myself as intellectually flawed. I still feel vulnerable and embarrassed when I ask questions, ashamed of not having the information other people seem to possess.

49

"I brought this background with me as I worked through the symposium. The men's words triggered the old sense of intellectual inadequacy. But this time, I was most aware of my body's reaction as I read their words. My body knows and understands, and it is from my embodied-knowing that I take on these men and their ideas. I felt nauseous, angry, and appalled at their blatant ignorance of women. I was shocked by the power they assumed and how out of line they were to use that power to define women.

"I wondered about the women who lived with these men. A dank and musty feeling swept through my body. I felt small, tight, claustrophobic, and trapped. It was hard to keep reading — and not because I didn't understand their words. I realize now that there are some words I no longer accept into my being. The healthy part of me shuts down and refuses to listen to words that deny my existence.

"I wondered why they used so many words and so much energy to convince themselves of our inferiority. My awe of women's power grew as I read their words because those men were threatened by our power, bodies, and influence over them. And respect for my own intelligence grew as I listened to my intuitive evaluation of their unacceptable words."

"The stigmatizing of Eve has caused vast harm over the millennia,
including the burning of thousands of wise spiritual women for "witchcraft"
and the array of man-made traditions and beliefs which treat the female body
as unclean and restrict girl's and women's agency to subordinate, inferior roles."
—Emily Jones, *The Girl Child's Long Walk to Freedom*

"We have to look more honestly and directly at what it means to call 'sacred'
such non-reformable biblical texts as the story of Adam and Eve."
— Pamela Milne, Associate Professor of Hebrew Bible, University of Windsor

# CHAPTER 4

---

## *The Idolatry of God the Father*
### Religious Trickle-Down

*Belief in the male god of traditional religion is mandatory,*
*like waiting for the prince and saying please and thank you.*
*But it's not natural—we are born free of belief.*
*—Patricia Lynn Reilly, Name Your Own Gods*

*Man enjoys the great advantage of having a god endorse the code he writes;*
*and since man exercises a sovereign authority over women it is especially*
*fortunate that this authority has been vested in him by the Supreme Being.*
*—Simone de Beauvoir, The Second Sex*

Religious images filled my childhood and adolescence. Although I saw many more images of Mary and Jesus than I did of god, his image was the most influential in my life. He was the unseen power behind the scenes. He was at the top—in the highest heavens. Every other image pointed to him, bowed to him, and owed its very existence to him. He was everywhere, they said, even in your mind, heart, and body. He could see your every thought and feeling, wish and dream. He knew your every move.

It felt scary to have a big stranger always there, always watching. After they told me about the all-seeing god, nothing was all mine, private and untouchable. There was no safe and quiet place that was my own. The image of an ever-present god is a shaming image that embodies the three essential ingredients of a shaming event:

- Exposure: God sees everything even the most private thought or feeling.
- Scrutiny: God searches the depth of our being to find sin.
- Judgment: God is the judge. His verdict is final. Arguing with god is not allowed.

Paradoxically, I was also taught that god was a loving god, yet his image seemed harsh, unlike Jesus who was gentle and kind, and loved little children. Yet Jesus' love could not erase the punitive nature of father god who sentenced his only begotten son to die on the cross. A sacrifice was essential in both Judaism and Christianity to atone for human sin. According to Christianity, Jesus was the final sacrifice. His blood was shed for the remission of our sins.

Hopeless and hell-bound, we were to turn to him for our salvation. Not only were there catastrophic consequences on a cosmic level for the sin of humankind, there were severe consequences for "walking away from god" after becoming a Christian. God punishes any deviation from his will. I "walked away from god" my sophomore year of high school. This took a lot of courage because I was stepping outside of god's protection and anything could happen to me. I didn't stay away from god for very long that time. The warnings, admonitions, and threats were effective. They kept me in line for years.

During high school and college, I was in a constant battle with my "natural" sensations, needs, desires, and capacities. It was my "natural self" that got me into trouble. Anything natural or spontaneous was to be "crucified with Christ." Driven to please god, an ever-increasing chasm existed between my natural, essential self and the artificially constructed Christian self that was necessary for acceptance within the church.

And finally, the most influential aspect of the image of god for women is "his" maleness. We were taught that god was greater than all of our attempts to enclose 'him' within a language. And yet there it is again . . . that male pronoun. Rather than employ a variety of names to more effectively illustrate the mystery of god, the teachers and preachers of our childhoods always used the male pronoun. Their words contradicted the lessons they taught us.

Religion had given god a man's name (and body) while claiming that god was beyond naming, that 'he' was a mystery. And yet, in the Catholic Mass we were confronted with at least 50 pronouns and images referring to god as male. And from the Hebrew Scripture and Protestant Bible read regularly in church or synagogue, we heard these popular gender-specific verses:
- "God rested from all his work which he had done in creation". (Genesis 2:3)
- "The Lord is my strength...and he has become my salvation; this is my father's God and I will exalt him." (Exodus 15:2)
- "For God so loved the world that he gave his only begotten son that whosoever believeth in him shall not perish but shall have everlasting life." (John 3:16)

## The Shadow of the Most High

Whether shouted at us in the religious institutions of our childhoods or whispered to us in the culture, the religious words and images of father god, judgment and punishment, unworthiness and shame, of a sinful Eve and an obedient Mary linger in our memories. Whether recited weekly in Sabbath School or experienced daily in the design of our parents' relationship, the religious myths of the exclusively male god, original sin, and the necessity of a male savior are deeply ingrained within women's lives. No matter how far we may have traveled from the religion of our childhoods, the image of the male god lingers within us. His image overshadows us even in our most private moments. It is his image that must be exorcised.

Patriarchal religion pursues us across the centuries of our cultural history.

The god of Abraham, Isaac, and Jacob; the triune god of Christianity; the Hebrew Scriptures and the Christian Bible; and the myths, stories, and rituals of religion are deeply ingrained in every aspect of the American social fabric. Our own personal stories are inextricably bound to the history, culture, and taboos of the world in which we live.

Patriarchal religion pursues us across the decades of our family history

Many of the life patterns, gender attitudes, and family customs that our families took for granted have their roots in religion's words, stories, and myths. There was no way to escape religion's pervasive influence in our childhoods.

> "It is the rare family that can trace back beyond two or three generations and not find that their predecessors were deeply immersed in the attitudes and values of one of the male-oriented religions. It is for this reason that religious pressures are not as far from us as we might prefer to think." —Merlin Stone, *When God Was a Woman*

Patriarchal religion pursues us into the seemingly ordinary interactions of our personal history. We carry the language and images of traditional religion with us into adulthood long after we may have discarded a particular set of religious beliefs. Engraved within the habits and ineffective behaviors that trouble us as adults are customs, attitudes, and expectations rooted in our religious past. I remind all women, even the most non-religious among us, that religious issues, questions, dilemmas, and concerns come up all the time:

- Awaiting word about the fate of a dying friend, we wonder if god will hear our prayers even though we haven't prayed to "him" for years.
- Discussing the pros and cons of getting married or "just living together" and of whether to baptize, confirm, or circumcise the children to please the extended family.
- Sitting in a Twelve Step meeting desperately wanting serenity and sobriety yet ambivalent about the prerequisite that we surrender to a higher power who sounds a lot like the childhood god we discarded years ago.
- Trying to describe our emerging spirituality to a friend and noticing our inability to articulate its depth and meaning without using the language of our religious past.

Religion powerfully affects every aspect of a woman's unfolding life whether it was an active participant in her development as it was in my life or a silent partner, providing the underpinnings for her development as it may have been in yours. It's impossible to fully understand our personal past if we don't explore the religious reality that shaped us all. Many of the life patterns, gender attitudes, family customs, and child-rearing practices that our families took for granted have their roots in the myths, dogmas, and stories of religion. There was no way to escape religion's pervasive influence in our childhoods and in the formation of the question "what's wrong with me." Imagine sitting in circle with these women. Add your story to theirs.

- "Although I grew up in an atheist home, I didn't escape the influence of religion. I married a Catholic and agreed to raise our children within his church. The book *A God Who Looks Like Me* confirmed my concern about the effect of religion on my daughter."

- "I do not have a religious background, and yet when I was asked to fill out a questionnaire about spirituality, I referred to god as 'he'. This surprised and troubled me. I wondered, "how did 'he' get in there." I thought about changing the pronoun to 'it,' but that felt blasphemous. The male god was embedded within me somehow."

We had no choice; the god of our childhood was male. Origen, an Alexandrian Church Father wrote these words in the third century: "What is seen with the eyes of the Creator is masculine, and not feminine, for god does not stoop to look upon what is feminine and of the flesh." Clearly, the architects of Western civilization (and its current defenders) attributed the male gender to the divine, supporting their belief in the superiority of the male — he looks like god and is looked at by god, and the inferiority of the female — she does not look like god and he does not stoop so low as to look at her.

It is useful, at this point, to invite Elinor Gadon, author of *The Once and Future Goddess*, to put the ascendancy of the male god into perspective: "The concept of monotheism is a relatively recent one, first expressed by the ancient Hebrews less than 4,000 years ago. The exclusive authority of one universal male god in Western culture reaches back to less than 1,700 years to the 320 CE conversion of the Roman Emperor Constantine and his imposition of Christianity as the state religion."

As we reviewed in Chapter 2, it took Christianity 6 centuries to successfully dethrone the Goddess by demoting her to mere saint, villain, or fill-in actress status within its altered myths. And since Constantine's consolidation of power in 320, Christianity has attempted to convert the rest of the world to its male-centered "one true faith." All the while, the Goddesses were stuck in mythologies that demeaned them, twisted out of shape by stories that disregarded them, and portrayed in ways that bore no resemblance to their original power and glory.

The worldview of the architects of western civilization is held firmly in place by monotheism's central belief in a male god who presides over a hierarchic reality. To fully understand our communal history and the current clamor for a return to the "old ways," we must deepen our understanding of religion's pivotal role in the development of Western civilization's historical, philosophical, theological, and psychological viewpoints (Chapter 3). The white male god is making a comeback and in preparation we can already hear his call for Jehovah's prophets and monotheism's armies to mobilize once again to annihilate all blasphemous notions of the Goddess and to put uppity women back in their place as secondary and subordinate.

## He Reigns Undisturbed

I have considered the question "what's the big deal about the gender of god" with audiences all over the country in bookstores, churches, and women's centers, and on radio and television interview and call-in programs. We consider the question in reaction and response to a performance piece entitled "Imagine" based on my first book. The performance invites audiences to imagine how their lives might have been different surrounded by images of the divine feminine in their churches, synagogues, and homes.

Through my Humanist ministry and by way of performances and presentations, I challenge the human community to confront its idolatry of god the father. The responses I receive illustrate the pervasive influence of the male god-image and the dangers of stepping outside the lines to question, reject, and redesign religion from a woman-affirming perspective. In Salt Lake City, Mormon men expressed outrage that women would even consider naming and imagining their own gods, "a blasphemous enterprise" was one caller's response.

A Utah Sunday School teacher and his class became concerned about me after reading an interview in a local paper. They sent me a stack of letters, inviting me to "come back to father God." The teacher rebuked me for encouraging women to create gods in their own image. "Lay down your pride and leave God alone" was his message to me. In Albuquerque, conservative Christian women and men called with similar outrage, name-calling, and concern that I find my way back to the one true god.

In Hayward, California, callers criticized the station for allowing such a blasphemous discussion to be aired. An Oakland caller assured me that her church would pray for my wayward soul. In response to a Boulder magazine interview, a flurry of letters attacked anyone who would question the male god of traditional religion. A Colorado man labeled our search for a god who looks like us "narcissistic feminism;" an interesting comment given the tenacity with which men have safeguarded the image of a male god, who looks like they do, for the past 4,000 years.

### Undisturbed in the Recovery Community

The male god also reigns undisturbed in the 12 Step community. Women, overwhelmed by their own addiction or caught up in the addiction of another, reach out to the Twelve Step community for assistance. The first step 'We admitted we were powerless over alcohol that our lives had become unmanageable,' is relatively easy for them to acknowledge because it is their obvious unmanageability that prompts them to seek out a community of support.

The second step 'We came to believe that a power greater than ourselves can restore us to sanity' is harder to accept. The god-talk of old timers feels like proselytizing to the newcomers. This "god-talk" triggers early attitudes, beliefs, and experiences with religion. Images of confessionals and Days of Atonement, pangs of guilt and shame, and the judgmental voices of rabbis and priests well up within them.

Yet they desperately need the support of the program so some women twist their god (or absence of god) into the shapes thought acceptable. Others stuff the religious images of childhood back into the closet to quiet the pangs of guilt and to silence the judgmental voices of old. Others leave the program unable to 'get the god-part'. Imagine sitting in a Deeper Wisdom Circle with recovery women and adding your story to theirs:

- "When I entered Adult Children of Alcoholics and read the second step, I was reminded of the early Catholic vision of God as the old father in the clouds with the long white beard and book of judgment. This image made me uncomfortable."
- "My response to the 'god-talk' of the program was mixed. One part of me was relieved to think I could rely on a power greater than myself. The other part of me was embarrassed to hear members speak of Christianity's God because it didn't offer me the comfort I yearned for as a child. Its messages were so contradictory."

## Undisturbed in the Psychotherapy Community

For many women, the therapist's office has replaced the confessionals of childhood. In times of crisis and stress, instead of reaching out to a minister or rabbi, they call their therapist for an appointment. Once the initial stress is relieved, their deeper questions often surface. They become aware of a spiritual dimension to life. Although they sense that religion and spirituality are distinct, they do not yet have the words to describe their emerging spirituality apart from the language of their religious past.

These women seek the guidance and support of their therapist to sort through their questions and to develop a personal spirituality. There are therapists who label such questioning 'religious' and therefore steer women away from their quest. These women feel trapped between their religious past and their present desire for a spiritual connection with little or no support from the therapeutic community. Add your story to theirs:

- "I worked with a counselor for several years who spoke of god occasionally. She always used 'he' to refer to this god and assumed that this was my understanding as well. I bristled every time she mentioned 'him.'"
- "The male god of my childhood was a partner in the dysfunction of my family, and yet when I would bring 'him' up, my counselor would redirect the discussion away from him. She seemed uncomfortable with religion. Being a good girl, I never challenged her."

In the Catholic and Protestant communities within which I was raised, prejudice against so-called "non-believers" went hand in hand with a mandatory belief in god. I was groomed to pity the nonreligious, to assume that they lived sin-filled lives, and to avoid association with them except when trying to convert them. This prejudice was not based on reason or actual experience—it was passed down. I inherited it. When I finally became curious and courageous enough to venture out beyond the insular bubble of religion, I was surprised by how nice everyone was.

> "In my neighborhood, we are made fun of because we don't go to church. Everyone says, 'I don't want you to go to hell,' as if hell is real. My family doesn't believe in hell, heaven, or god. We just want to be accepted for who we are and have fun with our friends. But they always bring up god." —Holland Openly Secular Alliance Survey

As an adult, I lived for a while in a Midwest community where god the father reigned undisturbed. Most residents were oblivious to their inherited prejudice, which manifested itself as Christian prayers at city council meetings, rocks thrown at non-religious students on the playground, Christian groups openly proselytizing in the public schools, and Christian crosses and symbols displayed in public spaces. All of the above manifestations of Christian privilege show preference for Christianity and in the process, marginalize other members of the community whose religious or secular beliefs are not represented or respected.

> "Last July, after years of patriotic Independence Day celebrations in the community park, the radio station sponsoring the event chose to feature an evangelistic Christian band with a proselytizing agenda. This meant that we were all subjected to their very specific religious message and music throughout the event. We were shocked, saddened, and upset, and have decided to stop attending." —Holland Openly Secular Alliance Survey

"God is male and that's a fact" sums up the response of many in this country. There is a big deal about the gender of god. "His" image and likeness have been woven into the history, philosophy, religion, and psychology that trickle down to us through the ages, a legacy passed on from generation to generation in the unexamined beliefs, customs, and preferences of a society that worships a male god and offers particular privileges to those who look like "him." God the father has remained an undisturbed idol for too long and sadly, any gains we've made in dismantling his legacy are being challenged of late.

## Trickle-Down in the Church

Church and family are patriarchy's primary delivery systems. This was bell hooks' experience: "When my older brother and I were born with a year separating us in age, patriarchy determined how we would each be regarded by our parents. Both our parents believed in patriarchy; they had been taught patriarchal thinking through religion. At church they had learned that God created man to rule the world and everything in it, and that it was the work of women to help men perform these tasks, and to obey. They were taught that God was male. These teachings were reinforced in every institution they encountered."

Religious Trickle-Down #1: So successful were the architects of Western Civilization, that there were no religious rituals in the churches of our childhood that celebrated the birthing powers of women. According to the religious myth we revisited in Chapter 2, the world was brought into being by a male god and woman was created from man. In a society that worships a male god, the boy-child's resemblance to the divine affords him power and privilege, and the father's life is more valuable than the mother's life.

> "Our mother was smarter and stronger than our dad. This was something we never dared to say out loud because everyone knows dads are supposed to be smarter and stronger than moms. We all had to pretend, including Mom, who pretended she didn't know what she knew and that she couldn't do what she could do." —Workshop Participant

Religious Trickle-Down #2: There were no religious rituals in the churches of our childhoods that celebrated the girl-child's birth. According to religion's myths and customs, the birth of the boy child was honored: Moses, John the Baptist, and Jesus, come readily to mind. On the other hand, the girl-child's birth was not announced and celebrated by angels, her arrival did not merit regal visitors and precious gifts, and in her honor the peoples of the world did not gather for a yearly exchange of generosity. In a society that worships a male god, sons are more important than daughters. Boys are groomed to administer the world. Girls are groomed to attract and take care of men.

- Psalm 127: "Sons are a heritage from the Lord, children a reward from him. Sons are like arrows in the hands of a warrior. Blessed is the man whose quiver is full of them."
- "As a child, I had a keen sense of being on the sidelines as a passive observer. I was expected to be ladylike. I was constantly compared to my male cousins. They weren't any more accomplished than I was, yet the conversations focused on them. My sisters and I were not as important in comparison." —Workshop Participant
- "To think that all in me of which my father would have felt proper pride had I been a man, is deeply mortifying to him because I am a woman." —Elizabeth Cady Stanton

Religious Trickle-Down #3: There were no religious rituals in our childhood churches that celebrated the flowing of a woman's blood. According to religion's myths and customs, the blood of sacrificed animals was ceremonialized and the blood of a male savior was honored. In a society that worships a male God, the girl-child's body and natural processes are messy, inconvenient, and 'other' than god. She is a 'misbegotten male' and the shame of her otherness accompanies her throughout life.

> Leviticus 15: "When a woman has her menstrual flow, she shall be in a state of impurity for seven days. Anyone who touches her shall be unclean 'til evening. Anything she lies or sits on during her impurity shall be unclean. Anyone who touches her bed shall wash his garments, and bathe in water, and be unclean until evening."

> "My great aunt wasn't allowed to dust the altar in the local Catholic Church while she was menstruating. The priest told her that her blood would pollute the altar. My cousin witnessed this monthly taboo and it served as her introduction to the curse of being female and the confusion about her own developing woman-body." —Workshop Participant

Religious Trickle-Down #4: Images of strong, self-contained women were exiled from the religious history we were taught. Images of passive women were elevated as the ideals to emulate. In a society that worships a male god, outspoken and independent men are applauded. Outspoken and independent women are called names and ostracized.

> "My aunt never married. She had a mind of her own and was considered off her rocker by the rest of the family. I wasn't allowed to spend too much time with her. They didn't want me to follow in her footsteps. But she was the happiest woman in the family, so why wouldn't I want to be like her?" —Reader

> "In my family and in the Catholic Church the prevailing opinions of my father and the male god could never be challenged. I remember remaining silent with my peers until I could sense their thoughts. Only then would I venture forth with an opinion that wouldn't rock the boat. Girls seldom risked expressing thoughts or opinions of their own. "—Reader

Religious Trickle-Down #5: Images of sexually autonomous women were exiled from the religious history we were taught. Images of chaste submissive women were elevated as the ideals to emulate. In a society that worships a male god, the boy-child's body is subject to uncontrollable sexual urges. The girl-child's body is vulnerable to these urges from birth. "Boys will be boys," even when they grow-up and marry. Girls are expected to be virgins before marriage and faithful to their husband in marriage.

> "In adolescence my mother was fearful about me "sleeping around." She believed that men liked.. virgins better. My mother referred to my brother's live-in girlfriend as a slut. Her standards were not equal. Influenced by the church, a woman's body was subject to much harsher scrutiny and judgment than a man's body was." —Workshop Participant

Religious Trickle-Down #6: There were no religious rituals in the churches or synagogues of childhood that celebrated the coming of the post-reproductive season of a woman's life. According to religion's myths and customs, it was the old men who presided at the sacred rituals of childhood in the home and house of god. In a society that worships a male god, the boy-child looks ahead to increased stature and wealth as he ages. The girl-child will be unprepared to grow old, and she will dread it.

> "I fear the isolation and rejection that go along with growing old as a woman. My mother serviced everyone and yet did not prepare a future for herself. She was ignored by our family (and the world) as she aged. The opposite was true for our dad." —Reader

The gender of god matters. "His" image and likeness are woven into the history, philosophy, religion, and psychology we inherit. This legacy is embedded within the unexamined beliefs, customs, and preferences of societies that worship a male god and offers special privileges to those who look like him. This legacy posits that the father is god, that his life is more valuable and his activities more important than the mothers. His privilege inflates his ego, threatening the planet's survival. His wars take precedence over the safety and education of children, the care and feeding of the hungry, and the common good of humanity.

Men are not the only ones threatened by our dismantling of the idolatry of god the father and reclamation of the divine feminine. I visited Canada to offer a critique of religion's exclusively male god-language and imagery and its effects on women's psyches, bodies, and lives. I stood before an audience of therapists, ministers, lay women and men, and Salvation Army officers. My opening words were:

> "Our imaginations have been held hostage by the male god. 'He' has been an undisturbed idol for too long. His image has been used to convince women that they are 'other' than god, inferior to men, and in need of a male savior."

As I was finishing my talk, two women walked out. I found out that they were offended by two words: "Woman God." We tread on dangerous ground when we call into question the exclusively male language and imagery used for the divine. The ground becomes even shakier when theologically arrogant women name their own gods, claiming the "supreme hubris of the god-makers" and asserting to ourselves the right to "reorder the world" and rename its gods.

Long after we discard our religious beliefs, they linger in our self-concept and contribute to the ineffective behaviors we bring into support groups, self-help meetings, and counselors offices. Now referred to as "Patriarchal Stress Disorder," these adaptive behaviors result from the chronic stress and anxiety many of us experience, navigating a world designed by and for men. The influence of religion, patriarchy's primary delivery system, cannot be ignored.

> "Basically, if you believe that a white man rules the heavens,
> you are more likely to believe that white men should rule on Earth."
> Steven O. Roberts, Assistant Professor of Psychology, Stanford

## Altar Boys, 1960

"If you have to wear a dress
to be an altar boy, why can't I be one?"
I asked the priest who said mass
at my elementary school.
"God is the father. He is a man, my dear,
only boys and men are allowed at the altar."

Years later I discovered the official reason
for my exclusion. My female body and
its processes, according to god, priest,
and pope, were considered immoral
and dangerous. That's why I could use
my body to clean the sacristy,
but I was considered unfit, and
thus banned, from being an altar server.

## Altar Boys, 2022

Low and behold, Pope Francis changed the law.
Women and girls are now allowed
to be "altar servers."

The Vatican made it clear, however,
that this expansion of roles
will never include ordained ministry
because a physical resemblance is required
between the priest and god.

In other words,
only boys can be priests—
they look like god, and girls don't.
Some things never change.

> "I had wanted to be part of that warm and wondrous world and they wouldn't let me.
> They had denied it to me because of a circumstance, because I was a girl. An injustice
> had been performed by a world that taught justice. Why should I continue to be part of
> something that behaved this way? How could I trust it?" —Chaim Potok, *Davita's Harp*

## A Pause Between Chapters
### The Apple

### Does the Bible name the Tree of Knowledge or the Forbidden Fruit?
"The Hebrew Bible does not specify what type of fruit Adam and Eve ate. It is described as simply the 'fruit of the tree' with no specific identification and no indication that it was an apple. The word used for the Genesis fruit was 'tapuach,' which means generic fruit." —Rabbi Ari Zivotofsky, Israel's Bar-Ilan University

### How did the fruit of the tree in Genesis become an apple?
"John Milton's 1667 poem *Paradise Lost* dramatizes the oldest story in the Bible, whose principal characters we know only too well: God, Adam, Eve, Satan in the form of a talking snake—and an apple. Except that Genesis never names the apple, but simply refers to 'the fruit.' But in the course of his over 10,000-line poem, Milton names the fruit twice, explicitly calling it an apple."
—Nina Martyrs, NPR, *"Paradise Lost and the Forbidden Fruit"*

### Why the forbidden fruit in Genesis is probably not the apple.
"It appears that people confused the Latin word 'malum,' which means 'evil' with the word 'malum', pronounced differently, which means 'apple' and somehow conflated the two meanings in the vernacular. The Byzantine Greek tradition, however, holds that the forbidden fruit was actually a fig."
—*Dr. Irene Lancaster, Jewish Academic, Author, and Translator*

"It wouldn't matter if tomorrow the old and new testaments were categorically debunked as historical frauds, because we inhaled their 'word of god-ness' based on the church's literal belief in and presentation of the stories, characters, and dictates found in that influential book." (From Chapter 1)

"For many of us the apple was a literal apple and Eve's bite was the forbidden bite and that bite catapulted all of humankind into suffering and death. Eve's story was shaped by patriarchy's foundational lies, which take up residence in our minds, hearts, and lives until they are dismantled intellectually, 'exorcised' theologically, and evicted from within our socialization." —Patricia Lynn Reilly

# CHAPTER 5

## An Encounter with Eve
### The Mother of All Living

*"The liberating encounter with God/ess is always an encounter*
*with our authentic selves resurrected from underneath the alienated self."*
—Rosemary Radford Ruether, *Sexism and God-Talk*

*"Men develop ideas and systems of explanation by absorbing past knowledge*
*and critiquing and superseding it. Women, ignorant of their own history do not know*
*what women before them had thought and taught. So, generation after generation,*
*they struggle for insights others had already had before them, resulting in the*
*constant reinventing of the wheel."* —Gerda Lerner, *The Creation of Patriarchy*

We reclaim the Mother of All Living by telling the truth of another time, a time when Goddess looked like us. We reach back to when her temples were extravagant; her writings, honored; and her symbols, revered. We reclaim our woman-history from the very beginning. We reclaim our Original Goodness by making known the unknown story that shadows the Bible and its development. We reclaim the life-affirming images of the very beginning. Listen as The Mother of All Living breaks out of traditional religious interpretation.

### An Encounter with Eve

Imagine for a moment that it didn't happen the way they told you in the church and school of your childhood. Imagine Eve walking among us. In the depths of your imagination, listen as she tells her entire story and reclaims her former glory.

> I am Eve, the Mother of All Living, culmination of creation.
> I hold and nurture life within me.
> In the fullness of time, I thrust and push life from me.
> And all that I have given birth to is good, it is very good.
> *Honor all that has been demeaned.*
> *Receive all that has been cast aside.*

I was once known throughout the world as the Mother of All Living. The wisest among you have always honored Me in your myths of beginnings. I have been called by many names: The Great Mother, Law-Giving Mother, The Bearing One, She Who Gives Birth to the Gods, Queen of Heaven, True Sovereign, Mother of the World, Queen of the Stars, Fertile One Who Births All Things. I was called Inanna in Ur; Ishtar in Babylon; Astarte in Phoenicia; Isis in Egypt; Womb Mother in Assyria, and Cerridwen among the Celts.

I was worshipped for many centuries before the God of the Hebrews was imagined into being. As men became threatened by My power and by My intimate involvement in the origins of all life, they swallowed My stories into their unfolding mythologies and twisted My truth. My original power and glory are hardly recognizable in the stories you heard about Me in the churches and homes of your childhood. The image of a father god ordering the world into being was firmly imprinted on your imaginations. Did you even notice the absence of the Mother?

According to the Genesis myth, I was born of the man, from his rib they say. I am outraged at this twisting of the truth. Who among you was not nurtured in My womb? Who among you has forgotten the source of your life? Jehovah was ignorant of his mother. In his foolishness he said, 'I am God. There is none beside me'. His arrogance has always troubled Me.

As the Mother of All Living, I exist before all things. From My body, all that is proceeds. Every mother who bears a child is the embodiment of Me. In her pregnancy, she holds and nurtures life within her. In her labor, she thrusts life from her. She is woman, strong and powerful. She is the Mother of all Living. I am outraged that woman's good strong body, containing all things necessary for life, and the body of Mother Earth, which receives back all good things to Herself, are objects of disgust and fear to be controlled and dominated in the Genesis story.

*Honor all that has been demeaned.*
*Receive all that has been cast aside.*
*The Mother is good. She is very good.*

I was given a pivotal role in men's developing mythology. They say that out of feminine weakness I ate the fruit and then seduced Adam. That I set in motion a series of events that resulted in our expulsion from the garden and the release of misery and death into the world. They say I am guilty, and that evil is grounded in my very existence and nature. I have been called the Devil's Gateway, the un-sealer of the forbidden tree, the first deserter of divine law, and the destroyer of God's image. Of me was written, 'From a woman was the beginning of sin and because of her we all die.' I will no longer carry the burden of humankind's guilt and shame nor the mis-representations of my worship.

In the very beginning, the sacred grove was the birthplace of all things. Its trees of knowledge and life were intimately connected to my worship. They were not my private property, nor did I wish to control humankind's access to their wisdom. We honored and cared for the trees of the grove. They held within them the secrets of life and the wisdom of the Earth and her seasons.

Hebrew tribes worshipped me in my sacred groves. Hebrew women followed me. Some, in the secret of their hearts. Others boldly rejected Jehovah and convinced their husbands to follow me. When King Solomon grew old, his wives turned his heart toward the Goddess. He did not remain loyal to Jehovah as his father David had done. He built hill-shrines in my honor. The myth-makers twisted the truth to serve as a warning to the Hebrew people not to visit my sacred groves nor to eat of the fruit of its trees. The most zealous of Jehovah's prophets cut down my groves and burned my priestess' bones.

To eat of the fruit of the tree was to become aware of life's seasons—its trouble and beauty, its gift and challenge, its joy and sorrow, and to embrace it all as good. In the woman Eve you catch glimpses of my former glory. She was eager, curious, and wise. And with her strength, she bit into life and the fullness of its possibility. They twisted her curiosity and courage into disobedience.

*Honor all that has been demeaned.*
*Receive all that has been cast aside.*
*The tree and its fruit are good. They are very good.*

The snake is my wise advisor, counselor, and the interpreter of dreams. Symbol of Sophia, of wisdom, the snake is the bearer of immortality. Life is renewed in the shedding of its skin. Worn on my forehead, held in my hands, and coiled around my body, the serpent has always been my special companion and the symbol of my life-renewing powers. The myth-makers recognized the importance of the serpent to me. My trusted advisor was no longer to be trusted. Our special connection was demeaned. Instead of trust, they placed enmity between me and the snake. And the interpreters of Scripture renamed the snake, devil, to be feared and crushed.

*Honor all that has been demeaned.*
*Receive all that has been cast aside.*
*The snake is good. It is very good.*

As the Mother of all Living, I pick the fruit of life. It is good and satisfies hunger. It is pleasant to the eye and offers well-being. It is wise and opens the way to self-discovery and understanding. Those among you who are curious, who lust for life in all its fluidity, dare with me. Bite into life and the fullness of its possibility. Eat at the good fruit of life.

Open to the depths of goodness within you. Believe in your goodness. Celebrate your goodness. Live out of the abundance of who you are as a Child of Life. Affirm the original goodness of your children and your children's children until the stories of old hold no power in their hearts.

*I am Eve, the Mother of All Living, culmination of creation.*
*I hold and nurture life within me.*
*In the fullness of time, I thrust and push life from me.*
*And all that I have given birth to is good. It is very good.*

---

Linger with Eve for a while. Take in her words. Breathe into the power of her truth. Allow her words to flow with each breath as a healing ointment, restoring your mind, heart, spirit, and body to your former glory as the daughter of Eve, the Mother of All Living. If moved, express your response in writing, dance, song, drawing, or movement.

---

### Eve, Our Champion

For over 1,700 years, women have been biting into the Genesis texts and reinterpreting them from a woman's perspective. Reclaiming our personal and collective her-story takes us back to the third century. Epiphanius, an early church father, wrote a scathing rebuke of the "heretical" Montanist sect because the women in that sect claimed Eve as their champion and inspired by her, assumed leadership roles, ignoring "the differences of nature."

> "They bring with them many useless testimonies, attributing a special grace to **EVE** because she first ate of the tree of knowledge. Women among them are ordained as bishops, presbyters, and the rest, as if there were no difference of nature. The apostolic saying escaped their notice, namely that: 'Man is not from woman but woman from the man;' and 'Adam was not deceived, but **EVE** was first deceived into transgression.' Oh, the multifaceted error of this world!" —Epiphanius

As we explored in Chapter 3, the "differences of nature" rationale for the secondary status of women is found in the writings of just about every architect of western civilization. Eve was their scapegoat and women were expected to carry her shame in the way they dressed, spoke, and walked, in the amount of space they inhabited, and the amount of food they ate. Sound familiar? Yes, their prohibitions trickle down and shape our relationship to our bodies, to the food we eat, to the clothes we wear, to the shame we experience as we age, and to the ever-present question we ask, "what's wrong with me."

Beginning with the unnamed women of the heretical Montanist sect, women have recognized that their destinies are inextricably bound to Eve's story, and that to reclaim themselves, they must reclaim her. These women laid the groundwork for us. Their rebellious spirits inspire our forbidden acts. Claiming Eve as our champion is another essential step on our journey of reclamation. She inspires us, as she did the Montanists, to reclaim sovereignty over our bodies, choices, and lives, and to take our rightful place in the human community. She speaks across millennia: "Release the shame. Bite into your life and the fullness of its possibility."

## Defenders of Eve
*Sisters, we remember you.*

Courageous women have also challenged the prevailing views about Eve (and women) by assuming their equality with the male translators, interpreters, and commentators of the Bible. I have included some of them in the following "Litany of Remembrance." The litany was inspired by Chapter 7 of Gerda Lerner's book *The Creation of Feminist Consciousness.* Emboldened by their courage, assert your right to reorder your religious, spiritual, or secular communities.

- Unnamed Montanist women (2nd Century)
  Assumed prophetic roles in the church. Claimed Eve as their champion.

- Isotta Nogarola (1418-66)
  Learned Renaissance woman, biblical commentator, and defender of Eve.

- Laura Cereta (1469-99)
  Humanist, mathematician, and defender of Eve.

- Jane Anger (16th century)
  Biblical commentator, pamphleteer and defender of Eve's superiority.

- Rachel Speght (17th century)
  Brilliant deconstructionist of misogynistic views and defender of Eve's equality.

- Ester Sowernam (17th century)
  Aggressive deconstructionist and defender of Eve as "the mother of all living."

- Mary Astell (1666-1731)
  Biblical commentator, who challenged the authority of Bible interpreters.

- Sarah Fyge (1669-1722)
  Banished from her father's house for writing a poem celebrating Eve's goodness.

- Sarah Moore Grimke (1792-1873)
  Feminist, abolitionist, and defender of Eve's equality, freedom, and intellect.

- Joanna Southcott (1750-1814)
  Defender of women who bring the knowledge of Eve's good fruit to humankind.

*"Sisters, we remember you. We celebrate your forbidden acts."*

## Claiming Intellectual Equality and Arrogance
### Dismantling The Question "What's Wrong With Me"

*Inspired by Eve, I walked through my communal/historical past, actively engaging the words and ideas of the architects of Western civilization that shaped the question "what's wrong with me" and provided the justification for my self-critical attitudes. I healed into the present as I assumed intellectual equality with their systems of thought and activated my intellectual arrogance to dismantle the question "what's wrong with me." I was supported by courageous women who have challenged the traditional "doctrines" of biology, history, psychology, and philosophy from a woman's perspective. Imagine these women waiting outside "The Symposium" (Chapter 3) to challenge the men's posionous words with the truth of a woman's life.*

### MARY WOLLSTONECRAFT (1759-1797)

<u>Biting into Rousseau's educational philosophy</u>, Mary Wollstonecraft, philosopher, social theorist, champion of women, and mother of two daughters reads from her *Vindication of the Rights of Woman*. A product of the Enlightenment, she considered lack of education to be the primary cause of women's social challenges. She championed equal educational opportunities for girls and in the process challenged Rousseau's misogyny:

> "Rousseau carries the arguments, which he pretends to draw from the indications of nature, still further, and insinuates that truth and fortitude, the corner stones of all human virtue, should be cultivated with certain restrictions, because, with respect to the female character, obedience is the grand lesson which ought to be impressed with unrelenting rigour. What nonsense! When will a great man arise with sufficient strength of mind to puff away the fumes, which pride and sensuality have thus spread over the subject! "

> "The prevailing opinion, that woman was created for man, may have taken its rise from the Biblical story; yet, it is presumed that very few, who have bestowed any serious thought on the subject, ever supposed that **EVE** was, literally speaking, one of Adam's ribs. The deduction must be allowed to fall to the ground; or only be so far admitted as it proves that man, from the remotest antiquity, found it convenient to exert his strength to subjugate his companion, and his invention to show that she ought to have her neck bent under the yoke, because the whole creation was only created for his convenience or pleasure . . . "

---

### ELIZABETH CADY STANTON (1815-1902)

<u>Biting into Biblical theology and exposing its fallibility</u>, Elizabeth Cady Stanton, founder of equal rights and suffrage associations, editor of the History of Women's Suffrage, and mother of seven children, reads from her introduction to *The Woman's Bible*. Its publication was a courageous act. In it, Stanton and her revising committee dismantled the question "what's

wrong with woman" by challenging the powers that be: divine authority in the heavens, centuries of male biblical interpretation, and ingrained church custom.

"From the inauguration of the movement for woman's emancipation the Bible has been used to hold her in the "divinely ordained sphere," prescribed in the Old and New Testaments. The canon and civil law; church and state; priests and legislators; all political parties and religious denominations have alike taught that woman was made after man, of man, and for man, an inferior being, subject to man. Creeds, codes, Scriptures and statutes, fashions, forms, ceremonies and customs of society, church ordinances and discipline all grow out of this idea.

"These familiar texts are quoted by clergymen in their pulpits, statesmen in the halls of legislation, lawyers in the courts, and are echoed by the press of all civilized nations, and accepted by woman herself as "The Word of God." So perverted is the religious element in her nature, that with faith and works she is the chief support of the church and clergy; the very powers that make her emancipation impossible.

"The canon law, Scriptures, creeds and codes, and church discipline of the leading religions bear the impress of fallible man, and not of our ideal great first cause, "the Spirit of all Good," that set the universe of matter and mind in motion, and by immutable law holds the land, the sea, the planets, revolving round the great center of light and heat, each in its own elliptic, with millions of stars in harmony all singing together, the glory of the creation."

---

## SIMONE DE BEAUVOIR (1908-1986)

Biting into Freud's psychoanalytic musings about women, Simone de Beauvoir, writer, philosopher, and feminist reads from *The Second Sex*. Although current feminist scholarship debates the merits of her work, thousands of American women experienced a profound awakening while reading *A Second Sex* during feminism's resurgence in the 1960s and 1970s. De Beauvoir dismantles the question "what's wrong with woman" by exposing the inferiority-based socialization of the girl-child and by offering girl-affirming vision of parenting as relevant today as it was in 1949.

"If the little girl were brought up from the first with the same demands and rewards, the same severity and the same freedom, as her brothers, taking part in the same studies, the same games, promised the same future, surrounded with women and men who seemed to her undoubted equals, the meanings of the castration complex and of the Oedipus complex would be profoundly modified."

"Assuming on the same basis as the father the material and moral responsibility of the couple, the mother would enjoy the same lasting prestige; the child would perceive around her an androgynous world and not a masculine world. If she was emotionally more attracted to her father, which is not even sure, her love for him would be tinged with a will to emulation and not a feeling of powerlessness; she would not be oriented toward passivity."

"Authorized to test her powers, she would not find the absence of the penis, compensated by the promise of a child, enough to give rise to an inferiority complex; correlatively, the boy would not have a superiority complex if it were not instilled into him and if he looked up to women with as much respect as to men. The little girl would not seek sterile compensation in narcissism and dreaming; she would be interested in what she was doing; and she would throw herself without reserve into undertakings."

---

## GERDA LERNER (1920-2013)

<u>Biting into recorded history's inherent bias</u>, Gerda Lerner, a founding member of National Organization for Women, professor of history, and one of the founders of the academic discipline of women's history reads from two of her pivotal books: *The Majority Finds Its Past* and *The Creation of Patriarchy*. She dismantles the question "what's wrong with woman" by challenging women and men to "think themselves out of patriarchy's" social organization and to imagine into being "a world that is truly human."

"Women's history asks for a paradigm shift. It demands a fundamental re-evaluation of the assumptions and methodology of traditional history and traditional thought. It challenges the traditional assumption that man is the measure of all that is significant, and that the activities pursued by men are by definition significant, while those pursued by women are subordinate in importance. It challenges the notion that civilization is that which men have created, defended, and advanced while women had babies and serviced families and to which they, occasionally and in a marginal way, contributed."

"As long as both men and women regard the subordination of half the human race to the other as "natural," it is impossible to envision a society in which differences do not connote either dominance or subordination. The feminist critique of the patriarchal edifice of knowledge is laying the groundwork for a correct analysis of reality, one which at the very least can distinguish the whole from a part. Women's History, the essential tool in creating feminist consciousness in women, is providing the body of experience against which new theory can be tested and the ground on which women of vision can stand. A feminist world-view will enable women and men to free their minds from patriarchal thought and practice and, at last to build a world free of dominance and hierarchy, a world that is truly human."

---

## MARYANNE CLINE HOROWITZ

*Biting into the inherent bias of Aristotelian biology*, Maryanne Cline Horowitz historian and professor reads from her essay "Aristotle and Women." She represents the arrogance of feminist scholarship, challenging the inalienable doctrine of "natural law" in every arena of male thought and dismantling it one idea, one theory, and one distortion at time.

"It is time for us to recognize that infiltrating Aristotle's erudition was a very common prejudice: an unquestioned belief that the female sex is inferior to the male sex. Further proof comes from the fact that he very cleverly argued to explain away apparent female superiorities . . . He concluded that females develop more slowly in the womb, but that after birth they pass more quickly through the stages of puberty, prime, and old age. Slowness in the womb, resulting from coldness, is interpreted as a defect, despite his recognition that colder embryos are less damaged. Quickness out of the womb is also interpreted as a defect resulting from female weakness: . . . 'for all inferior things come sooner to their perfection or end, and as this is true of what is formed by Nature.'

"Women can't win with the supposed "empiricist;" all apparent differences between male and female are attributed to the "natural deficiencies" of the female sex.' Aristotle's complexity and accomplishment indicate his overriding concern for scientific and philosophical truth. What we must recognize is that the truth discovered was not neutral, but value-ridden. The inferiority of the female sex was not in Aristotle's works an explicit end-point, a doctrine to be proved or justified, but rather a value-ridden premise underlying his logical arguments on other topics. It is not enough that he gets his due from womankind, womankind must also get her due."

---

AUDRE LORDE (1934-1992)

Biting into women's self-negation and exposing its origins, Audre Lorde, lesbian, poet, and feminist theorist reads excerpts from her essay "Uses of the Erotic: The Erotic as Power." Her life and writing inspire us to expose and extricate every remnant of oppression from within and around us, and to view every personal choice we make for health, inclusivity, and freedom as a political act.

"There are many kinds of power, used and unused, acknowledged or otherwise. The erotic is a resource within each of us that lies in a deeply female and spiritual plane, firmly rooted in the power of our unexpressed or unrecognized feeling. As women, we have come to distrust that power which rises from our deepest and non-rational knowledge. We have been warned against it all our lives by the male world, which values this depth of feeling enough to keep women around in order to exercise it in service of men, but which fears this depth too much to examine the possibilities of it within themselves."

"But the erotic offers a well of replenishing and provocative force to the woman who does not fear its revelation, nor succumb to the belief that sensation is enough. When we begin to live from within outward, in touch with the power of the erotic within ourselves, and allowing that power to inform and illuminate our actions upon the world around us, then we begin to take responsibility to ourselves in the deepest sense. For as we begin to recognize our deepest feelings, we begin to give up, of necessity, being satisfied with suffering and self-negation, and the numbness which so often seems like the only alternative in our society. Our acts against oppression become integral with self, motivated and empowered from within. "

---

## ELINOR GADON (1925-2018)

Biting into god, Elinor Gadon, art historian and professor reads from *The Once and Future Goddess*. She challenges women and men of the late twentieth century to dismantle the idolatry of God the father and to reclaim ancient female images of the divine.

"Merlin Stone began her ground-breaking book with the revelation that in the beginning God was a woman, and so she was. Accumulating archaeological evidence affirms overwhelmingly that prehistoric peoples worshipped a female deity. This evidence and the earliest writings document the persistence of Goddess religion for nearly 30,000 years, beginning in the Late Paleolithic, the Ice Age. With the coming of agriculture, in the Neolithic Age that followed, the religion of the Goddess flowered."

"Goddess religion was earth-centered, not heaven-centered; of this world, not other worldly; body affirming not body-denying; holistic not dualistic. The Goddess was immanent, within every human being, and humanity was viewed as part of nature, death as a part of life. Her worship was sensual, celebrating the erotic, embracing all that was alive. The religious quest was above all for renewal, for the regeneration of life. The Goddess was the life force."

---

## bell hooks (1952-2021)

Biting into patriarchy, bell hooks, groundbreaking feminist critic, poet, and intellectual wrote about love, feminism, white supremacy, forgiveness, and the power of art. She challenges us to step into self-sovereignty. Her outrageous books include: *Ain't I a Woman: Black Women and Feminism and Feminism is for Everybody: Passionate Politics*.

*From Understanding Patriarchy*: "Patriarchal gender roles were assigned to all of us at birth and we were given continual guidance about the ways we could best fulfill those roles."

"Patriarchy is a political-social system that insists that males are inherently dominating, superior to everything and everyone deemed weak, especially females, and that males are endowed with the right to dominate and rule over the weak and to maintain that dominance through various forms of psychological terrorism and violence."

*From Feminism Is for Everybody*: "It's important to have a sharp, ongoing critique of marriage in patriarchal society because once you marry within a society that remains patriarchal, no matter how alternative you want to be within your unit, there is still a culture outside of you that will impose many values on you whether you want them or not."

"If any female feels she needs anything beyond herself to legitimate and validate her existence, she is already giving away her agency and power to be self-defining. The one person who will never leave us, whom we will never lose, is ourself. Learning to love our female selves is where our search for love begins. The moment we choose to love we begin to move against domination, against oppression. The moment we choose to love we begin to move towards freedom, to act in ways that liberate ourselves and others."

## A Deep Breath

The outrageous words of Mary Wollstonecraft, Elizabeth Cady Stanton, Simone de Beauvoir, Gerda Lerner, Maryann Horowitz, Audre Lorde, Elinor Gadon, bell hooks, along with the poetry of Susan Griffin, Virginia Wolf, Marge Piercy, Alicia Ostriker, and Ntozake Shange escorted me through my historical past to dismantle the question "what's wrong with me." These women supported me to claim intellectual equality with the traditions I had been taught to revere as untouchable and god-ordained. Thank you, brave women!

It is always in the company of women that we are reminded of our common heritage as women. A heritage that reaches beyond "the beginning" defined by men to the "very beginning" when the divine was imagined as woman. We discover that we are surrounded by a courageous cloud of witnesses—their experience and stories, ideas and images, and creativity and outrage become healing resources for us. No longer asking the question "what's wrong with me," we are freed from our obsession with the needs, mandates, and words of men. Self-possessed, we step outside of patriarchal thought and immerse ourselves in women's history, philosophy, theology, creativity, activism, and spirituality.

We have been warned against exhibiting hubris ("arrogant pride") all of our lives. The "outrageous words" of our feminist, womanist, 3rd WAVE, and international sisters support us to be arrogantly full of ourselves for the salvation of a planet out of balance and in danger of annihilating itself. In their every word, we hear the powerful affirmation, "It is right and good that you are woman. Be full of yourself!"

> One by one they step up and speak
> the truth of a woman's life
> told with heart, mind, and body
> refusing dissection

they are women and poets and theorists
who gather our brokenness
into their words
an impulse toward wholeness
awakens within us
and we become again
as we once were . . . whole.

---

## Claiming Theological Equality and Supreme Hubris
### Exorcising The Question "What's Wrong With Me"

*Inspired by Eve, I walked through my religious past, actively engaging the sin-based words, images, experiences, and expectations that shaped the question "what's wrong with me" and gave authority to my self-critical attitudes. I healed into the present as I assumed theological equality with the traditional doctrines of religion and activated my "hubris" to exorcise the question. I am supported by Eve who committed the forbidden act of breaking out of traditional religious interpretation and telling her own story.*

While in graduate school, I reread the Bible from my perspective as a woman free of the religious trappings of childhood and adolescence. No longer fearful that I would be damned for tampering with "God's Word," I began to assume equality with this very human book. I gathered the fragments of women's stories from my religious memory and from the margins of the text itself. I invited the women of old to visit my dreams and to tell me their stories. I also re-wrote some of the stories I identified with, changing the gender of the characters if necessary, inserting the specifics of my story into the text.

I found myself drawn again to the story of the man possessed by demons in Mark: 5. At that point in my life, I felt possessed by alien energies in the form of childhood's critical words, images, experiences, and expectations. They had taken on a life of their own, pursuing me into adulthood and dictating the terms of my existence without my consent. Raging within me, their force could no longer be contained. I was in need of a metaphorical exorcism.

I rewrote the Mark 5 story and have continued to interact with it over the years as I journeyed toward self-possession in the company of women from every age. Critical words, images, experiences, and expectations lodge within us as alien energies, cluttering our inner landscape. They become our inner accusers and must be "exorcised" on our way back to self-possession.

I dwell among the tombs. I was often fettered and chained, but was able to snap my chains and break free of the fetters. I could no longer be controlled. No one is strong enough to master me. And so, unceasingly, night and day, I cried aloud among the tombs and on the hillsides and cut myself with stones.

When I saw the Healer approaching my hiding place among the tombs, I came out of hiding and flung myself down before HER, shouting loudly, "What do you want with me, Healer? Do not torment me." The Healer asked: "What is your name?" I answered: "My name is Legion; there are so many of us."

The Healer turned toward me with a strong and loving gaze. She invited me to name the alien energies that cluttered my inner landscape. I named each alien energy, clothed as the ancient words and images that lingered within me:

Original sin. Universal sin. Hereditary sin. Actual sin. Venial sin. Mortal sin. Unpardonable sin. Unforgivable sin. Ultimate sin. Deadly sins. *"OUT," she commands.*

Eve is the instigator of evil. It was Eve's fault. It all goes back to Eve. Born evil. Born sinful. Born wayward. Atone for Eve's sin. Evil to your core. Completely, irrevocably flawed. *"OUT," she commands.*

Children are naturally wicked, willful, and sinful. Parents must punish and reward. Spare the rod and spoil the child. *"OUT," she commands.*

God is always watching. One can never escape God's wrath. Damnation. Go to hell. Sin. Sinner. Unworthy. Wretched. Missed the mark. Unclean heart. *"OUT," she commands.*

Bless me, Father for I have sinned. Imperfect. Inadequate. Shortcomings. Impure thoughts. Never quite good enough no matter what I do. Rise above all it all to perfection. *"OUT," she commands.*

God is everywhere, in my mind and heart and body. God sees every thought and feeling, wish and dream. God watches my every move. God searches the depth of my being to find sin. God is the judge. *"OUT," she commands.*

The Healer addressed Legion, "OUT, alien spirits, come out of this woman!" The alien spirits, clothed as ancient words and images, came out of me, one by one. Exhausted I fell to the ground. When I awakened and the Healer asked me again: "What is your name?"

"I am Daughter of Woman," I answered.

"Rise up and go into the night," said the Healer.

"Go to the circle of women. They will tell you more of the truth."

I rose up and went into the night. In its darkness, my eyes rested. The Moon called to me. She told me of a time when a woman's life was sacred. When there were no shameful separations. She told me of a time when a woman's body was honored. When there was no painful touch. I found myself in a clearing of light with women from every age. Their song called to me. "You who stand apart come close. You who are out of touch come near." They did not throw stones, instead they offered me flowers and anointed me with healing light. They sang to me: "It is right and good that you are woman." And they told me stories from the *very* beginning. Stories of ancient beliefs in a Great Mother who gave birth to the cosmos and its inhabitants, both human and divine.

> Stories of ancient times when it was from the Mother, the giver of life, that the line of the generations was traced; when women were honored for both their capacity to nurture and to accomplish great things; and when virginity meant "woman, complete in herself," owned by no man, creator of her own destiny.

> Stories of ancient women who did not apologize for their fertile wombs, pregnant bellies, full breasts; who honored the body of Goddess in their changing bodies; and who refused to surrender except to their truest self, wisest voice, and the natural rhythms of Life.

> Stories of ancient ways that honored a woman's blood as magic, flowing in harmony with the moon; that celebrated the accumulation of a woman's years and her wisdom; and that elevated the Crone as the one who presided at sacred rituals because she held within her generations of wisdom and depths of pain.

Women of all ages told stories in the light of the moon. In their stories, I heard my truth. In their dance, I shed my veil of shame. It is right and good that I am woman, that I was madwoman, and now I am whole.

The town's people came out to see what had happened. They encountered me, the one who had been possessed by a legion of alien spirits, now sitting clothed and in my right mind. The news spread about my healing.

As the Healer was leaving, I asked her, "May I go with you?"
"No," the Healer responded, "Go home to your own folk and tell them that once you were divided against yourself and now you are whole."

I returned home and spread the good news: "It is right and good that I am Woman, that you are Woman. There is no blemish in us." And all were amazed.

---

After the Exorcism:
• Some women place the papers on which they recorded the critical religious words, images, experiences, and expectations in a wok or fire circle. They burn them in silence and bury the ashes in their yard or garden while singing, "Since I Laid My Burdens Down"

## Claiming Personal Sovereignty
Reversing The Question "What's Wrong With Me"

*Inspired by Eve, I walked through my personal past, actively engaging the patriarchal "reversals of value" embedded within my fractured family's experience, reversals that shaped the question "what's wrong with me" and that taught me the language of self-criticism. I healed into the present as I assumed personal sovereignty and responsibility for my transformative journey and reversed the question by reclaiming my inner wisdom and natural capacities. I am supported by my deep commitment to the health and sanity of our daughters, granddaughters, and nieces, who in the very beginning of their lives, are full of themselves!*

We hold every memory, impression, image, word, event, and formative belief of childhood within us. Nothing has been lost or forgotten. It is impossible to ignore the past. It will always make itself known in troubling physical symptoms and persistent ineffective behaviors, as well as in the "splattering" of our unexamined memories and unreleased feelings on both our colleagues and political opponents. In order to be an effective and responsible agent of transformation in the culture, we must walk through our personal past.

Cognitive understanding alone does not reach to the depths of our self-critical attitudes. We do not remember our childhoods in nice neat developmental categories. We hold the memories and impressions of childhood in our bodies and sensations; in our tears, trembling, and joy; in the depth and pace of our breath; and in the repetitive and critical self-talk that accompanies our days. Reaching to these depths prepares us for a profound transformation of our inner world, a complete reversal of all we have been taught to believe about ourselves.

### The Journey
Our life journey has been described in a variety of ways by secular, religious, and philosophical systems of thought. Because religious beliefs have been central to traditional understandings of birth, life, death, and afterlife, the male god and those who look like him are considered the centerpiece of the life journey. Therefore, their needs, experiences, and well-being are at the center of what we learn about the human experience. They are the main event—we are secondary and supportive. They are the "A," we are the "B."

My understanding of our life journey was inspired by Eve's story and by two very special seven-year-old friends. They are exquisite young adults now—in their childhood they were my teachers. They reminded me of a time in the very beginning of my life when I was full of myself. As we spent time talking, singing, playing, and exploring together, snapshots of that earlier time passed through my mind's eye, fragments of a forgotten time.

Yes, in the very beginning of her life the girl-child is full of herself. Her days are meaningful and unfold according to a deep wisdom that resides within her. It faithfully orchestrates her movements from crawling to walking to running, her sounds from garbles to single words to sentences, and her knowing of the world through her sensual connection to it.

Her purpose is clear: to live fully in the abundance of her life. With courage, she explores her world. Her ordinary life is interesting enough. Every experience is filled with wonder and awe. It is enough to listen to the rain dance and count the peas on her plate. Ordinary life is her teacher, challenge, and delight.

She trusts her vision of the world and expresses it. With wonder and delight, she paints a picture, creates a dance, and makes up a song. To give expression to what she sees is as natural as her breathing. And when challenged, she is not lost for words. She has a vocabulary to speak about her experience. She speaks from her heart. She voices her truth. She has no fear, no sense that to do it her way is wrong or dangerous.

She is a warrior. It takes no effort for her to summon up her courage, to arouse her spirit. With her courage, she solves problems. She is capable of carrying out any task that confronts her. She has everything she needs within the grasp of her mind and imagination. With her spirit, she changes what doesn't work for her. She says "I don't like that person" when she doesn't, and "I like that person" when she does. She says no when she doesn't want to be hugged. She takes care of herself.

Three Seasons of Life

As I celebrated the remarkable capacities of my young friends, I became aware of critical words from my childhood and adolescence, echoing across the decades to challenge their fullness, and my own. These deeply imprinted words recount what happened to the precious being I once was, we once were, in the very beginning of our lives. Over time, the inner voice that led us into wonder-filled explorations was replaced by critical voices.

As a result, the girl-child's original vision is narrowed; she sees the world as everyone else sees it. She loses her ability to act spontaneously; she acts as expected. Her original trust in herself is shattered; she waits to be told how to live. Her original spunk is exiled; she learns that it is dangerous to venture outside the lines. Her original goodness is twisted and labeled unnatural-unfeminine-too intense-evil by the adults in her life.

As we explored in Chapter 2, she will grow up asking, "what's wrong with me?" This question regularly punctuates women's lives as they search for someone to give them an answer, for someone to offer them a treatment or cure. We have learned a criticism-based way of perceiving ourselves and relating to the world. As a result, our automatic tendency is to feel inadequate, that we are never quite good enough no matter what we do.

There are a variety of templates for understanding our life cycle. Using the phrase "Maiden, Mother, and Crone" to delineate the stages of a woman's life is helpful, but it is defined by our gender-specific roles and our relationships to others. Women long for a focus on their own lives and on the evolution of their unfolding self-understanding, apart from their "functions and attachments." Inspired by Eve and my young friends, I believe that a woman's life journey takes her through three distinct seasons. Each season is outlined here and expanded upon by insightful writers and teachers. Notice the similarities between our three-fold personal journey and the historical journey we have taken with Eve:

- In Season 1, Eve was the Mother of All Living and gave birth to All That Is.
- In Season 2, Eve was twisted out of shape by patriarchy. Born of Adam's rib and therefore assumed to be inferior, she becomes the "B" to Adam's "A."
- In Season 3, Eve is restored to her former glory as we, inspired by her, reclaim her story and reorder the world for the sake of our daughters!

---

Season 1      The Very Beginning: Our Natural Endowment

In the very beginning, the girl-child loves herself—and she is shameless. She comes into the world with feelings of omnipotence, not inferiority. She loves her body, expresses its needs, and follows its impulses. She recognizes and expresses her feelings. She tells the truth. She is interested in herself and enjoys private time. She is involved with herself and her own pursuits. She celebrates herself and expects acknowledgment for her creativity and accomplishments. This is the season, often short-lived, when girls have access to the resources and capacities necessary to support resilient living.

> "At the buried core of women's identity is a distinct and vital self, first articulated in childhood." — Emily Hancock, *The Girl Within*

> "Prior to adolescence girls are vital, resilient, and immune to depression. They have a clear sense of themselves and their character." —Carol Gilligan, *In a Different Voice*

> "I have a strong connection to my daughter. She reminds me of the girl child I once was. She is perfect. I look at her and don't see any flaws. She reminds me of my true nature. As I parent her as I wish I'd been parented, the child in me is healed."—Erin Stewart

---

Season 2      Forgetting: Conformity-Based Dictates

This is the season when the weight of patriarchal socialization takes a tragic toll on the girl child's organic unfolding. Sometime around adolescence she begins to understand that there is a script she is expected to follow. As a result, the pressure to conform veils her original self-love and replaces it with self-criticism.

According to *The Confidence Code for Girls*: "Between the ages of 8 and 14, girls' confidence levels fall by 30 percent. At 14, when girls are hitting their low, boys' confidence is still 27 percent higher. And the effects can be long lasting. During this season, many of our daughters become 'formula females.' And sadly, many will stay stuck in this season, wearing costumes and spouting scripts fashioned by a society that prefers men.

"Our psychological being has been severed from our biological selves for so long that we are completely cut off from our true natures." —Elinor Gadon, *The Once and Future Goddess*

"Adolescence is the most formative time in the lives of women. Girls are making choices that will preserve their true selves or install false selves. Their choices have implications for the rest of their lives." —Mary Pipher, *Reviving Ophelia*

"We found children at a very early age—from the most conservative to the most liberal societies—quickly internalize this myth that girls are vulnerable and boys are strong and independent." —Robert Blum, Director of the Global Early Adolescent Study (2017)

"When you grow up as a girl, the world tells you the things you are supposed to be: emotional, loving, beautiful, wanted. And then when you are those things, the world tells you that those things are inferior, illogical, vain, and empty." —Erika Villani, *The Virgin Suicides as a Novel of Female Adolescence*

"Simone de Beauvoir believed adolescence is when girls realize that men have the power and that their only power comes from consenting to become submissive adored objects. They do not suffer from the penis envy Freud postulated, but from power envy." —Mary Pipher, *Reviving Ophelia*

"Many teenage girls suffer from a crippling lack of self-esteem. All-encompassing insecurities are so commonplace within this demographic that society fails to register them as a problem. In fact, the media regularly and remorselessly vilifies teenage girls for characteristics that the patriarchy instilled in them." —Rachel Card, Writer

"By the time they are seventeen many young women have surrendered their ambitions to a growing need for affection and their autonomy to an emotional dependence on the approval and good will of others. At seventeen the young woman is well on her way to being a formula female." —Madonna Kolbenschlag, *Kiss Sleeping Beauty Goodbye*

"I stood at the grocery checkout near where clothing is sold in a boy's and a girl's section. The boy's section featured a sweatshirt with a wolf silhouette and the word "Leader." The girl's section featured a sweatshirt with a kitten saying the words, "Be Nice." Hard to believe that in 2022 this is still the way girls and boys are socialized." —Class Member

"In almost every society, from Baltimore to Beijing, boys are told from a young age to go outside and have adventures, while young girls are encouraged to stay home and do chores. In most cultures, girls are warned off taking the initiative in any relationship and by 10 years old, already have the distinct impression that their key asset is their physical appearance." —Belinda Luscombe, Time Magazine Editor at Large, "Kids Believe Gender Stereotypes by Age 10, 2017 Global Study Finds."

---

Season 3      Remembering What We Once Knew | The Return Home

In this season we wake up from the patriarchal trance, from Season 2's existential limbo, and reunite with our essential self and natural endowments. The wake-up call is often clothed as a revelation—my revelation was described in Chapter 1. The revelation invigorates the two essential tasks of this Season: Task 1-Reclaiming our self-sovereignty. Task 2-Relearning how to be, live, act, and love from the inside out.

"The liberating encounter with God/ess is always an encounter with our authentic selves resurrected from underneath the alienated self." —Rosemary Radford Ruether, *Sexism and God Talk: Toward a Feminist Theology*

"Virgin means One in Herself; not maiden inviolate, but maiden alone, in herself. To be virginal does not mean to be chaste, but rather to be true to nature and instinct." —Nor Hall, *The Moon and the Virgin*

"There was a time when you walked alone, full of laughter. You bathed bare bellied. You say you have lost all recollection of it, remember! You say there are not words to describe it; you say it does not exist. But remember! Make an effort to remember! Or failing that, invent." —Monique Wittig, _Les Guerilliers_

"Transformation comes from looking deep within, to a state that exists before fear and isolation arise, the state in which we are inviolably whole just as we are. We connect to ourselves, to our own true experience, and discover there that to be alive means to be whole." —Sharon Salzberg, *Voices of Insight*

"When we live from within outward, in touch with our inner power, we become responsible to ourselves in the deepest sense. As we recognize our deepest feelings, we give up being satisfied with suffering and self-negation, and the numbness, which seem like our society's only alternative." —Audre Lorde, *Sister Outsider*

"Your healing task is not to become a new, improved, or changed person. Rather, it is to heal into the present by reclaiming your natural and essential self in all its fullness. In the very beginning, you loved yourself." —Patricia Lynn Reilly, *Home is Always Waiting*

## Re-Socialized unto Self-Sovereignty

Each book and resource I have written reminds women of these three seasons and invites them to return home to the "very beginning" when they loved themselves. This "returning" involves ousting the question "what's wrong with me" from our hearts, minds, and bodies. Instead, we affirm that we are originally blessed, not cursed, and that strength, goodness, and creativity reside within each of us. We discover that the good is generous enough to embrace our mistakes and ineffective behaviors.

Claiming Eve as our champion is an essential step on our journey of reclamation. She inspires us, as she did the Montanists, to reclaim sovereignty over our self-understanding, bodies, choices, and lives, and to take our rightful place in the human community. She challenges us to reclaim our lives and the fullness of life's possibility.

To prepare for the next step on the journey (Chapter 6), I want to clarify that, in this book, the terms autonomy and self-sovereignty are synonymous. Here's a review of their similarities:

• AUTONOMY is the concept of property in one's own person, expressed as the natural right of a person to have bodily integrity and to be the exclusive controller of one's body and life.
> Synonyms: choice, free will, self-determination, self-ownership.
> Example: *"Economic autonomy is still a long way off for many women."*

• SELF-SOVEREIGNTY is the state of being free from the control of another. It includes freedom from external control or influence, and the power of making one's own choices and decisions.
> Synonyms: autonomy, freedom, independence, liberty, sovereignty.
> Example: *She left home and felt she'd achieved sovereignty for the first time in her life.*

Use the word that inspires you the most on your journey of reclamation. I personally have a preference for "self-sovereignty" because, as I shared in Chapter 1, Elizabeth Cady Stanton became a powerful mentor to me. She, along with many other writers, poets, and activist women, inspired me to reclaim my own self-sovereignty. This most powerful gift, given to us by life itself, was stolen from us by way of the indoctrination many of us received. In her own words, Stanton shared the reason she was an advocate on behalf of women's self-sovereignty:
> "The strongest reason why we ask for woman a voice in the government in which she lives; in the religion she is asked to believe; and equality in the social life, where she is the chief factor; is because of her right to self-sovereignty; because as an individual, she must rely on herself."

Inspired by Stanton, I used a "self-sovereignty" lens to reconsider the stories of Eve, Lilith, and Mary. I realized that each of our Mythic Mothers invite us to commit our own "forbidden acts" by seizing the gift of our self-sovereignty from the grip of patriarchy—a task fueled by our own personal authority. Clearly, self-sovereignty is central to each of their stories.

**EVE**, inspired by her curiosity and self-sovereignty, committed the "forbidden acts" of communing with the snake, picking a piece of fruit from the Tree of Knowledge, and taking a forbidden bite out of it. She invites us to claim our right to be free from the control of another and to make our own choices and decisions. (Chapter 5)

**LILITH**, inspired by her self-respect and self-sovereignty, committed the "forbidden act" of refusing to assume what was considered the inferior position during coitus with Adam. She reminds us of our natural right to have bodily integrity and to be the exclusive author of our story and life. In Chapter 6, we meet Lilith and explore the moment in history when Eve and Lilith's stories intersect.

**MARY**, inspired by her concern for ordinary people and their everyday triumphs and troubles, committed the "forbidden act" of refusing to stay in her place and becoming the accessible Goddess. She defined her own mission and accomplished it in spite of patriarchal belittlement and confinement. She continues to visit her followers around the world. In Chapter 7, we meet Mary and explore how she and Eve were pitted against each other in service of the patriarchal narrative.

## The Apple Communion

Inspired by Eve's forbidden act, our women's circle prepared a tribute to Eve and her courage. Clearly, her BITE was a courageous expression of self-sovereignty. Twisted out of shape by men, her BITE became the centerpiece of patriarchy's belief in the inferiority, shame, and subordination of women. It was a powerful BITE heard around the world and felt throughout the generations, bringing with it catastrophic consequences for girls and women.

Reader 1: The Invocation

*Imagine hearing Eve's words introducing this communion service:*

"As the Mother of all Living, I pick the fruit of life. It is good and satisfies hunger. It is pleasant to the eye and offers well-being. It is wise and opens the way to self-discovery and understanding. Those among you who are curious, who lust for life in all its fluidity, dare with me, bite into life and the fullness of its possibility."

Reader 2: The Apple Communion

*Imagine the elder women of the congregation handing an apple to the first person in each row.* As the crone hands you an apple, she looks into your eyes and says, "Take and eat of the good fruit of your life. Savor its sweetness and share its blessing. It is right and good that you are woman." Imagine biting into the apple, savoring its sweet juiciness, and then passing it on to the person next to you with the same words.

Reader 1: The Goodness Blessing

> There is nothing wrong with you. Open to the depths of goodness within you. Believe in your goodness. Celebrate your goodness. Live out of the abundance of who you are as a child of life. Affirm the original goodness of your children and grandchildren until the stories of old hold no sway in their hearts. Imagine biting into life and the fullness of its possibility.

Read by All Present: A Declaration of Self-Sovereignty

> My thoughts are my own. I will not modify them to receive the approval of others.
> My feelings are my own. I will not silence them to make others comfortable.
> My body is my own. I will not allow others to twist it out of shape.
> My life is my own. I will not shape it according to the expectations of others.
> I live in harmony with my natural cycles, deepest wisdom, and truest self.

> This is it. This is my life. Nothing to wait for.
> Nowhere else to go. No one to make it all different.
> What a relief to have finally landed here, now.
> Blessed be my life!

### Jenny's Story: "This Could be Scary"

"After sorting through the Adam and Eve story with Patricia, our women's group passed a basket of apples around the circle. As we each took a piece of fruit, I suddenly realized we were going to take a bite, just like Eve. I hesitated—original sin was a long time ago and it was not my fault, but if I reenact the BITE, does that make me BAD? Now I understood my friend's words, "This could be scary." But then I thought about how serpents and goddesses used to be considered "good" and how self-serving the Genesis story really was. I finally took a bite and it felt empowering. The apple was delicious, and I was surrounded with support."

> *Until we imagine something, it remains an impossibility.*
> *Once imagined, it becomes our experience.*
> *Imagine a woman who bites into her own life and the fullness of its possibility.*
> *A woman who has opened to the depths of goodness within her.*
> *Who affirms the original goodness of her children until the stories*
> *of old hold no sway in their hearts. Imagine yourself as this woman.*

# CHAPTER 6

## *An Encounter with Lilith*
### The Rebellious First Woman

*"The battle isn't waged by waiting patiently, or hoping patriarchy will come to its senses and finally relinquish its power. It's waged by unlearning what patriarchy teaches, expects, and rewards for good girls." Mona Eltahawy, The Seven Necessary Sins for Woman and Girls*

*"When women understand that governments and religions are human inventions; that Bibles, prayer-books, catechisms, and encyclical letters are all emanations from the brains of man, they will no longer be oppressed by the injunctions that come to them with the divine authority of "Thus saith the Lord." —Elizabeth Cady Stanton*

As the face of god changed in my experience, I searched for images of strong women. My search led me to a remarkable publication. In 1898, The Woman's Bible was published by a group of women who were outraged by the inaccurate interpretations of the Bible used to support women's inferior position in home, church, and society. Written by Elizabeth Cady Stanton and her Revising Committee, the Woman's Bible is composed of a series of commentaries and essays dealing with portions of the Bible that had the most impact on the lives of women, either in its degraded portrayal of them or in the glaring absence of their stories and concerns.

The creation and publication of *The Woman's Bible* was a courageous act. In it, Stanton and her committee challenged the powers that be: divine authority in the heavens, centuries of male biblical interpretation, and ingrained church custom. Their look at the Bible from a woman's perspective in 1898 offers us empowering insights as we, in 2022, search through its pages for glimpses of a god who looks like us.

As a result of her forbidden act of challenging the infallibility of the Bible, Elizabeth Cady Stanton became alienated from the Women's Rights movement to which she had committed her astounding gifts and tenacious activism. She could no longer tolerate the reluctance of the religiously conservative suffrage movement to "take an advanced step" of challenging religion's entrenched misogyny. Exhilarated by her soon to be realized freedom, she wrote: "Once out of my present post in the suffrage movement, I am a freelance to do and say what I choose and shock people as much as I please."

Stanton eventually joined the Women's National Liberal Union because its positions were more in line with her growing skepticism toward all religions. Speaking truth to power, the most stunningly accurate resolution put forth by the National Liberal Union read: "That Christianity is false and its foundation is a myth, which every discovery in science shows to be as baseless as its former belief that the earth was flat."

"The untold story of the feminist movement is that it was sparked and nurtured by the religious non-conformists and liberals, by the unorthodox and heretics, by the freethinking skeptics, rationalists, agnostics, and atheists." —*Women Without Superstition*

## In the Beginning: Two Stories

From The Woman's Bible we learn that there are actually two accounts of the creation of female and male recorded in Genesis. In the first account, man and woman were created simultaneously in the image of Elohim (plural god). In the second, woman was created from the man and named by him. Which one did you hear in childhood?

### A Simultaneous Creation: Genesis 1: 26, 27, 28

26: And Elohim (plural god) said, "Let us make them in our image, after our likeness: and let them have dominion over the fish of the sea, the fowl of the air, and the cattle, and all the earth, and over every creeping thing that creeps upon the earth."

27: So Elohim (plural god) created male and female in their own image, in the image of Elohim created he them; male and female created Elohim them.

28: And Elohim (plural god) blessed them, and said unto them, Be fruitful and multiply; and replenish the earth and subdue it; and have dominion over the fish of the sea, over the fowl of the air, and over every living thing that moves upon the earth.

### Woman from the Man's Rib: Genesis 2: 18, 20-23

18: Then the Lord God said, 'It is not good for the man to be alone. I will provide a partner for him.' (God then created animals and birds, and gave man the task of naming them.)

20: But for the man no partner had yet been found.

21: And the Lord God caused a deep sleep to fall upon Adam, and he slept; and he took one of his ribs, and closed up the flesh thereof.

22: And from the rib which the Lord God had taken from man, made he a woman, and brought her unto the man.

23: And Adam said, 'This is bone of my bone, flesh of my flesh: she shall be called woman because she was taken out of man.'

In the first account, man and woman were created simultaneously by Elohim (male-female /plural god) and both were to have dominion over the Earth. In the second account, woman was created from the man and named by him. Elizabeth Cady Stanton summarizes the differences this way: "The first account dignifies woman as an important factor in creation, equal in power and glory with man. The second makes her a mere afterthought. The world in good running order without her. The only reason for her advent being the solitude of man."

The second account has been favored throughout Hebrew and Christian history. Its dominance reflects centuries of male control of the teaching, preaching, and interpretive tasks in the church. From the male perspective, its preference may make perfect sense. From a woman's perspective, it was a tragic choice—a myth passed on from one generation to another in song, story, and image, convincing generation after generation of girl-children of their inferiority, and limiting their dreams and the expression of their gifts in the world.

Although in the churches of our childhood, there was no acknowledgment of the inherent contradictions in the two Genesis stories, there have been many attempts to make sense of them by scholars who could not ignore the glaring discrepancies. Centuries before Stanton and her committee, rabbis who studied and interpreted the Scripture to make its insights relevant to succeeding generations assumed that god made several attempts to fashion a suitable mate for Adam. Thus, two stories.

Genesis 1, according to these rabbinical commentators, records god's first attempt, which proved unsuccessful and required a second try which is recorded in Genesis 2. According to the rabbis' legend, a rebellious woman named Lilith was Adam's first wife. Because she refused to assume what was considered the inferior position during coitus with Adam, she was eventually replaced by Eve, a more docile substitute.

The rabbis borrowed material from the oral traditions, stories, legends, sayings, and folk tales of surrounding cultures. They reworked this material and wove it into their commentaries. Because the Goddess was worshipped in the surrounding culture, as we explored in Chapter 2, remnants of her stories found their way into Hebrew myths and interpretations. And because the rabbis were men, immersed in a male-dominated world view, their use of Goddess imagery was distorted, and negative images of women abound.

Originally, Lilith was a Sumerian Goddess called the 'Divine Lady'. Her roots reach into ancient Mesopotamia, dating back to 2300 BCE. She was honored as the assertive and sexually self-possessed wild spirit of the night. By the time she finds her way into the rabbinical legend as Adam's first wife in the 10th century AD, her story had been twisted out of shape. She was stripped of her divinity and had become a demonic image to be cast out. To dilute her power, she was called demeaning names and to dilute her popularity, cautionary tales were fabricated, warning women not to emulate Lilith or her daughters, the "Lilim."

## An Encounter with Lilith

In the brave tradition of *The Woman's Bible*, we ask Lilith, the legendary first woman, to break out of the confines of religious interpretation to retell her story in her own words, incorporating the healing images from the very beginning when the divine was imagined as woman.

I am Lilith. I doubt that you've heard much about me.
My story didn't make it into the scripture.

*In the very beginning,*
there was Darkness. It flamed forth in power.
It asserted itself and I was created.
In the image of the Moon was I brought forth.
I reach toward the Depths.

*In the very beginning,*
there was Light. It flamed forth in radiance.
It asserted itself, and the Sun was created.
It reached toward the Heights.

Darkness and Light were equal in dignity.
Moon and Sun shone equal in splendor.
Depth and Height were held equal in respect.

*In the beginning,*
There was a dispute.
The Light feared the Darkness and its power.
The Sun feared the Moon and its night.
The Heights feared the Depths and its unknown.

The Light swallowed the Darkness.
The Sun swallowed the Moon.
The Heights swallowed the Depths.
The old ways were almost forgotten.
New stories were written.

According to the rabbis, the Breath of Life and the Dust of Earth formed me and Adam. We were created from the same source so I expected full equality with him. He did not agree with me on that and other matters. He demanded that I serve him and that I lie beneath him when we made love. I was outraged.

With the help of 'The Name That Is Not to Be Spoken', I flew away. I vanished into thin air and settled at the Red Sea. Adam complained to God, who sent three angels after me. Their attempts to capture me were fruitless. I prefer living alone to life with the man.

My story is very simple. Remembering my former glory before I was swallowed into the rabbis' commentary, I refused to be mistreated by man or god. I did what any self-respecting

woman would have done. I said, 'Enough is enough,' and I left. Here are a few of the names they've called me and the stories they've told about me over the centuries:

They call me **Spinster** because I live alone and am perfectly content. I refuse to allow men to hold me in check. They do not understand so they call me names.

They call me **Night Hag**, not to be confused with ugly, mind you. Some thought my daughters and me so beautiful and so expert at lovemaking that after an experience with us, a man was never again satisfied with mortal women.

They call me **Whore, Harlot, and Seducer.** Celibate monks tried to keep me away by sleeping with their hands over their genitals, clutching a crucifix. Men say I distract them from their progress toward personal salvation. Eve is the wife, the faithful woman. I am a seducer.

They call me **Tormentor of Men**. Although my story disappeared from the Bible, my daughters, the Lilim, are said to have haunted men for thousands of years. Well into the Middle Ages, Jewish men were manufacturing magic charms to keep my daughters away. We supposedly appear at night and exert magical powers over young men. They say we cause nocturnal emissions.

Woven into my reputation are men's deepest fears of impotence, weakness, and isolation in the face of my unfettered female sexuality, assertiveness, and independence. All that I represent threatens them, so they call me names.

They call my refusal to be submissive and subordinate...rebelliousness.

They call my assertiveness in taking care of myself... bitchiness.

They call my independence of men...unfeminine.

They call my sexuality, unconnected to a husband...unnatural.

I am tired of their names!

Woman, is it any wonder you have feared me? They convinced you that all that I represent is evil, unnatural, and unfeminine. Is it any wonder that you exile me from within you?

---

Linger with Lilith for a while. Take in her words. Breathe into the power of her truth. Allow her words to flow with each breath as a healing ointment, restoring your mind, heart, spirit, and body to the truth. A truth that reaches back to before men named and labeled us, to the very beginning. If moved, respond in writing, dance, song, drawing, or movement.

---

## *Reversing the Girl-Child's Socialization*

As we explored in Chapter 5, there is a time in the very beginning of her life when the girl-child is acquainted with the Lilith within her. At the age of nine, a majority of the girls in a survey of 3,000 were confident and assertive, and felt positive about themselves. Sadly, that first season of a girl-child's life is often short-lived. Unless there is an intervention, by the time she's 10 the girl-child will have forgotten her Lilith-like qualities.

According to the 2017 global study we reviewed above, girls at 10 are already cautious about taking the initiative in any relationship and already have the distinct impression that their key asset is their physical appearance. The girl-child will emerge from adolescence with a poor self-image, relatively low expectations of life, and much less confidence in herself and her abilities than the boys have.

Although men and women alike are encouraged and rewarded for conforming to the norms of the society in which we live, for women, these norms are particularly restrictive. The norms will continue to tighten around the lives of girls and women if theocracy is the outcome of our current cultural and political upheavals. She will be discouraged from owning the fullness of her power, courage, or independence. In her book *Reviving Ophelia*, Mary Pipher lists the setbacks that occur during the transition from Season 1 (birth to 10) to Season 2 (adolescence):

> "Many young women are less whole and androgynous than they were at age ten. They are more appearance-conscious and sex-conscious. They are quieter and more fearful of holding strong opinions. They are more careful what they say and less honest. They are more likely to second-guess themselves and to be self-critical. They are bigger worriers and more effective people pleasers. They hide their intelligence. Many must fight for years to regain all the territory they lost."

Born into a world that prefers men, the girl-child learns early to twist herself into the acceptable shapes of church, family, and culture. Convinced that our Lilith superpowers are unfeminine and unnatural, she will exile her Lilith-like qualities. In the company of women, we take our first step toward reclaiming Lilith by acknowledging the societal and religious realities that shape the girl-child, and then reversing them to reflect the truth of the girl-child's life. We are supported on this journey by remembering a time that once was . . .

> We recall ancient times when women were honored for both their strength and their tenderness, for both their capacity to nurture and to accomplish great things.

> We reclaim ancient ways that taught women to refuse submission and subordination, applauded women for their assertiveness, and encouraged women to be independent.

> We reawaken ancient beliefs in a strong and capable Goddess who was trustworthy; who acted on behalf of all women; who did not apologize for her power, courage, and independence; and who could say, 'Enough is Enough' and make it so.

## Lilith's Resistance: Power, Courage, and Independence

Mary Pipher reminds us that "resistance keeps the true self alive." The most powerful way to assist our daughters and granddaughters, and ourselves, to hold on to our true self and original resilience is to reverse patriarchy's socialization. How do we do that?

1. Know Patriarchy, Inside and Out: We deepen our understanding of patriarchal socialization within our own experience and as it relates to our daughters and granddaughters. We convey to our daughters an understanding of patriarchy, using creativity and age-appropriate examples. In Mary Pipher's experience that process also includes "discovering the personal impact of cultural rules on women, discussions about breaking those rules and formulating new, healthy guidelines for the self." This knowledge becomes our daughter's north star and her magic sword and shield.

2. Cultivate Self-Knowledge: We encourage the girl-child to grow in self-knowledge and to make regular conscious contact with her "truest self" through the mindfulness skills now being taught in many schools and homes. She must know that her "inner home" is hers alone and that it will always be available to her. We must assist her to formulate strong affirmations of her worth, strength, power, courage, and individuality. These consciousness skills become her refuge and her strength.

3. Cultivate Self-Reflection: We equip the girl-child to critically distance from any socialization and/or indoctrination experience that doesn't feel right to her. This skill gives her the space and time necessary to untangle what's going on and to determine what her response needs to be. This "situational analysis" capacity becomes another one of her super-powers.

4. Identify Super-Powers: In her work with girls, Mary Pipher discovered some of their resiliency super-powers. Smart girls, independent girls, and girls considered unattractive, "although socially isolated and lonely in adolescence," eventually experienced their isolation as a "blessing because it allowed them to develop a strong sense of self. Girls who are isolated emerge from adolescence more independent and self-sufficient than girls who have been accepted by others." Thus, intelligence, independence, and isolation can turn out to be lifesavers for our daughters. At the same time, Mary Pipher's observations challenge us to remain aware enough of the dynamics of our daughters' socialization that we are able to assist them in navigating the seasons of their lives.

5. Normalize Resistance: Power, courage, and independence are three of the qualities that both give birth to and enable our resistance. One way to normalize resistance is to introduce our daughters to role models who are already exhibiting these essential qualities. In the next section three young women will be introduced. They have accomplished powerful outcomes with their own unique blends of power, courage, and independence. By hearing their speeches, reading their books, and joining their powerful campaigns, our daughters become acquainted with strong female words and powerful female voices. Each of these young women, in her own way, has become a world-changer and system builder. Instead of sitting down and shutting up, they stood up and spoke out. They reversed the patriarchal mandate. They are free!

## *Reclaiming Power*

### Our Original Power: Seasons 1 and 2

In Season 1 of her life, the girl-child is acquainted with the powerful Lilith within her. She is capable of carrying out any task that confronts her. She has everything she needs within the grasp of her mind and imagination. She accomplishes great things in the solitude of her own mind and heart, and orchestrates creativity projects and lots of adventures in the neighborhood. The power of the universe pulsates through her. She is full of herself.

In Season 2, the girl-child feels the weight of patriarchal socialization and its expectations. There are those who are threatened by the girl-child's Lilith-power and attempt to squash it. They will call her names if she insists on owning her power. She is told, "Proud and Uppity One, don't get too big for your britches. Pretend you can't do it so the boys will help you. You'll never be a CEO, priest, or god. The world's a big and scary place for Little Red Riding Hood. Eve's daughters are small, weak, and powerless."

Eventually the powerful one falls asleep. Occasionally she awakens to a faint memory of her childhood power. These periodic reminders are painful. She fills her life with distractions so she will not hear the quiet inner voice calling her to return home to her own power.

### We Reclaim Our Power: Season 3

Working with sexual assault survivors, I struggled to find an empowering feminine image that would awaken their own inner power. Many had been encouraged to embrace power in the form of 'the masculine within them.' This is an inappropriate, disempowering, and triggering image for those who have experienced sexual exploitation at the hands of men.

The centrality of an admission of powerlessness in self-help philosophies also disturbs me. Men and women bring different experiences to the concept of power. For men to acknowledge their powerlessness means relinquishing the illusion of power with which they have been saturated since childhood. This admission allows them to seek significant connection and mutually supportive relationships within a spiritual or recovery context.

On the other hand, women have been admitting powerlessness most of their lives. Our access to thrones, negotiating tables, board rooms, pulpits, and presidencies has been limited. Our inferior position has been clear. Thus, the admission of powerlessness, as it has been defined by men, is not woman-affirming. What we need to do instead is reclaim our original power.

As women recognize the Lilith within them, they redefine power as the capacity to act on their own behalf, author their own lives, and deal with whatever situation confronts them. For men, the admission of powerlessness is essential in order to experience connection with others. For many women, walking into their first therapy appointment, women's support group, or recovery meeting is a powerful act on their own behalf.

Lilith reminds our daughters (and ourselves) of what we once knew in the very beginning of our lives. Inspired by Her and together with our daughters, we affirm our original power:

> I am capable of carrying out any task that confronts me. I have everything I need within the grasp of my mind and my imagination. I accomplish great things in my home and neighborhood, and in the world.

> I am Proud and Uppity One. I am too big for my britches. I do not need the boys' help. I will be a doctor or a mother or a priest or whatever I want to be. I am capable. The power of the universe pulsates through me. I am full of myself.

## Power: A Role Model for Our Daughters

Inspired by the POWER of Emma Gonzalez, the girl child will be able to visualize what it means to act and speak with POWER. Inspired by her friends who had been shot and killed in her Parkland, Florida high school, Emma became a powerful advocate for gun control. Each of her speeches reflected the force of her grief, which intensified every word she spoke. Her "We Call BS" speech went viral, calling for "gun control" advocacy and empowering young people to speak out against school shootings.

In 2018, the Florida Legislature passed the "Marjory Stoneman Douglas High School Public Safety Act." The act allocated millions to raise the minimum purchase age to 21; to establish waiting periods and background checks; and to provide a program to arm teachers and hire school police. Rick Scott signed the bill into law with these words: *"To Marjory Stoneman Douglas High School students: You made your voices heard and fought until there was change."*

By getting to know Emma, our daughters and granddaughters will be inspired to confront patriarchy in all its manifestations. Resisting patriarchy's gun violence in the schools, churches, homes, and streets of our communities becomes an option for the use of their Lilith POWER.

---

## Reclaiming Courage

### Our Original COURAGE: Season 1 and 2

In Season 1 of her life, the girl-child is acquainted with the courageous Lilith within her. She is a warrior. Whatever the difficulty, she knows there is a way to face into it. It takes no effort for her to summon up her courage, to arouse her spirit. With her courage, she solves problems. With her spirit, she changes what doesn't work for her. She says no when she doesn't want to be hugged. She says 'I don't like that person' when she doesn't, and 'I like that person' when she does. She takes care of herself. The courage of the universe pulsates through her.

In Season 2, the girl-child feels the weight of patriarchal socialization and its expectations. There are those who are threatened by the girl-child's unique courage and will attempt to preach it out of her. They will call her names if she refuses to submit. If she says enough is enough, she is told, "Stubborn and Angry One, say yes when you mean no. Give your anger to god. Forgive. Stay. Stick it out. Fulfill the higher purpose to love, honor, and obey. Pain and suffering are necessary to a woman's life. Bear your husband's bad ways in a spirit of penance. Eve's daughters are passive."

Eventually, the courageous one falls asleep. Occasionally she awakens to a faint memory of her childhood courage. These periodic reminders are painful. She fills her life with distractions to quiet the inner voice calling her to return home to her courage.

### We Reclaim Our COURAGE: Season 3
Lilith supports women to take action on their own behalf and to expect equality in their relationships. Not only was she twisted out of shape by male-dominated religion into a demon who terrorized men, her story was twisted into a warning to rebellious wives not to leave abusive situations. We refuse the twisted patriarchal version of Lilith's story by reclaiming her story from the very beginning. She took care of herself. She said, 'Enough is enough' and refused to be mistreated by god or man.

Lilith inspires us to embrace our anger and to act with strength on our own behalf. She gives us the courage to leave abusive situations. In every aspect of our lives, Lilith encourages us to "Be Powerful. Be courageous. Exert, initiate, and move on your own behalf." Imagining such a mother, Fiona wrote: "Every aspect of my life would have been better. I would have a much stronger idea of who I am today because all of these exertive commands would have pushed me to know myself, test myself, experience myself, and be active in the world."

Lilith reminds us of what we once knew in the very beginning of our lives. Inspired by Her, together with our daughters, we affirm our original courage:
- I am a warrior. Whatever the difficulty, I know there is a way to face into it. It takes no effort for me to summon up my courage, to arouse my spirit. With my courage, I solve problems. With my spirit, I change what doesn't work for me.
- I take care of myself. I say no when I don't want to be hugged. I say 'I don't like that person' when I don't. I say 'I like that person' when I do.
- I am Stubborn and Angry One. I leave when I want to. I refuse pain and suffering. I am active. The courage of the universe pulsates through me. I am full of myself."

94

Inspired by the COURAGE of Malala Yousafzai, the girl child will be able to visualize what it means to act and speak with COURAGE. In the face of threats on her life, Malala continued to go to school in a country that does not want girls to be educated. One day, those who oppose the education of girls stopped Malala's school bus and shot her. She survived and continues to work on behalf of the world's girls. She tells her own story in her book *I Am Malala: The Story of the Girl Who Stood Up for Education and Was Shot by the Taliban. Here's an excerpt:*

> I was born in Mingora, Pakistan on July 12, 1997. I spoke out publicly on behalf of girls and our right to learn. And this made me a target. In October 2012, when I was 15 years old, a masked gunman boarded my school bus and shot me on the left side of my head. I woke up 10 days later in a hospital in England. The doctors and nurses told me about the attack and that people around the world were praying for my recovery.
>
> After months of surgeries and rehabilitation, I joined my family in our new home in the United Kingdom. It was then I knew I had a choice: I could live a quiet life or I could make the most of this new life I had been given. I determined to continue my fight until every girl could go to school. With my father, who has always been my ally and inspiration, established the Malala Fund, a charity dedicated to giving every girl an opportunity to achieve a future she chooses. In recognition of our work, I received the Nobel Peace Prize in December 2014 and became the youngest-ever Nobel laureate.

By becoming acquainted with Malala, our daughters and granddaughters learn to speak up and change the world with COURAGE. They become equipped to use their own courageous words and actions to confront patriarchy in all its manifestations. Supporting the education of girls becomes one option for them to courageously resist patriarchal violence against girls.

---

## Reclaiming Independence

### Our Original INDEPENDENCE: Seasons 1 and 2

In Season 1 the girl-child is acquainted with the independent Lilith within her. She is pregnant with her own life. It is her virgin time. She is content to be alone. She touches the depths of her uniqueness. She loves her mind. She expresses her feelings. She likes herself when she looks in the mirror. The solitude of the universe pulsates through her. She is full of herself.

Some are threatened by the girl-child's unique independence and they attempt to scare it out of her. In Season 2, they call her names if she chooses a life of her own. She hears these patriarchal messages: "Selfish One, your time, energy, and attention are to be used in service of others. You are to wait for the One who will come. It is most important that you are desirable—prepare your body and face for his coming. Your real life begins when the deliverer arrives." Eve's daughters are always waiting."

Eventually, the independent one falls asleep. Occasionally she awakens to faint memories of her childhood independence and freedom. These periodic reminders are painful. The young woman fills her life with distractions so she will not hear the quiet inner voice calling her to return home to her own independence.

## Reclaiming Our INDEPENDENCE: Season 3

Generations of girl-children have been crippled in the expression of their lives because the images of strong, self-contained women have been exiled from religious history. The women's stories that were read in the churches and synagogues of childhood were designed to cultivate and reinforce our helplessness. Convinced of the customary, the girl-child doesn't even consider the option of a solitary life. A life alone is portrayed as a curse, something to be avoided at all costs. It takes tremendous courage for the girl-child to create an original life that is not centered on a relationship.

Rather than twist herself out of shape, Lilith left the customary path and entered the territory of her own experience. Some of us choose to follow her. We travel as she did to the 'far away' place to get to know ourselves. We choose to be alone, whether for an hour a day, a weekend a month, or for a full season of our lives. Whether we are in a significant relationship or not, we take time to nurture and replenish our spirits. In our solitude, we relearn the lessons of Lilith, the Independent One. We are reminded of our personal dreams and goals. We develop a relationship with our inner resources.

Lilith preferred life alone to life with a partner. With her encouragement, some of us reclaim this as an option. Inspired by her courage, we choose abstinence from sexual and romantic relationships for a month, a year, or a lifetime. In our abstinence we deepen our contentment and satisfaction with our own lives. We reclaim our abundant inner resources. We develop a firm commitment to our own true potential. Lilith reminds us of what we once knew in the very beginning of our lives. Inspired by Her, together with our daughters, we affirm our original independence:

> I am pregnant with my own life. This is my virgin time. I am content to be alone. I touch the depths of my uniqueness. I love my mind. I express my feelings. I like myself when I look in the mirror. My body and face are my own. I am desirable to myself.

> I am Selfish One. My time, energy, and attention are used in service of my own life and projects that call to me. I change my life if I want it changed. I will no longer wait for someone to make my life matter. My life begins anew each moment. The solitude of the universe pulsates through me. I am full of myself.

Inspired by the **INDEPENDENCE** of Greta Thunberg, the girl-child will be able to identify her values and visualize what it would mean for her to act and speak with authenticity, creativity, and independence in service of those values. At 15, worried about her future and the future of the planet, Greta stood alone outside the Swedish Parliament every day for three weeks during school hours. Her sign read, "School Strike for the Climate." No longer alone, Greta's commitment to her values inspired millions of students around the world to join her in protesting the inaction of the world's leaders on climate change.

In the face of intense bullying and threats on her life, Greta continues to act up on behalf of the world's young people whose very lives and futures hang in the balance as adults refuse to act immediately to address climate issues. Greta has come out as "autistic" and wrote/spoke these powerful words without apology, without artificial politeness, and without offering respect to adults who do not deserve it:

> "Yes, I have Asperger's Syndrome and that means I am sometimes a bit different from the norm, but given the right circumstances, being different is a superpower. In many ways we who are autistic are the normal ones and the other people are pretty strange. They keep saying that climate change is an existential threat and the most important issue of all. And yet they just carry on like before. If the emissions have to stop, then we must stop the emissions. To me that is black or white. There are no grey areas when it comes to survival. Either we go on as a civilization or we don't." —Greta Thunberg

By becoming acquainted with Greta, our girl-children learn how to act up and speak out for something they believe in, even if that means standing alone to get the job done as Greta did. Inspired by Greta, they will use their own **INDEPENDENCE** and uniqueness to confront patriarchy in all its manifestations. Fighting for the dismantling of our fossil-fuel based infrastructure becomes one option among many for dismantling patriarchal dominance over Mother Earth, their home.

---

## Reclaiming Our Wholeness

We have given voice to the experiences of childhood that convinced us that our power, courage, and independence are unfeminine and unnatural. We have retrieved the collective story of women from the margins of history and religion. We have designed a strategy to assist our daughters and granddaughters to understand patriarchy and to stand up to it with their words, actions, and voices.

And with courage, we have retold Eve and Lilith's stories, incorporating the healing images of a time when the divine looked like us. As the Mother of All Living and the Rebellious First

Woman meet within us, we recover our original capacity to nurture and to take assertive action. Lilith represents our capacity for independent assertive action. Eve, the Mother of All Living, represents our intimate involvement in the origins of life.

Inspired by a time that once was, when women were honored for both their capacity to nurture and to exert, we imagine Lilith wandering at the edge of the garden. She meets Eve, the woman who replaced her. We imagine Eve and Lilith sharing a piece of fruit and exchanging stories. They play in the Earth and re-imagine their beginnings. The Earth is their womb. In the fullness of time, they are born again of Mother Earth. They name themselves.

> *Eve declares:*
> I am the Mother of All Living, culmination of creation.
> I hold and nurture life within me.
> Welcoming is my womb. Nurturing, my love.
> In me, you are enclosed and sustained.
>
> Lilith declares,
> I am the Rebellious First Woman.
> Strong is my womb. Powerful its thrust.
> In the fullness of time, I push life from me.
> In me, you exert, initiate, and move.
>
> In one voice, we speak across the centuries,
> We were woman divided. Now we are one.

## In Gratitude for New Images

At "Our Mythic Mothers" retreats, we create a collage of gratitude to Eve and Lilith. They have become healing images for us as we welcome home the exiled aspects of ourselves. Imagine sitting in a circle of women and acknowledging the gifts you have received:

> "As I descend into my Lilith-self, I am reclaiming my power. I no longer look to men to be assertive for me. I am powerful and accomplish great things."

> "I am drawn to Eve. I have a lot of driving energy within me. I am always pushing myself. I never rest. I imagine Eve as an abundantly warm and round woman. I want to crawl into Her roundness and be held. I want to feel that I am loved for just being. I would like to rest for a while."

> "I am grateful for a mythic female role model who symbolizes the qualities of assertion and initiative often associated with men. Her image has made going about the business of getting what I want professionally less difficult and painful. It is invaluable to realize that these aggressive characteristics are also feminine."

"I am grateful Eve and Lilith are not idealized objects of pleasure or Hollywood goddesses. They are assertive and powerful women who encourage me to honor who I am apart from my relationship and to embrace both the passive and pushy energies within me. I am both nurturing and self-confident. These qualities are not mutually exclusive."

"Lilith pushed me to re-discover the creative and outward person I once was. My first major in school was drama. Yet as an adult, I have been anorexic as far as accomplishment is concerned. I've stayed in frustrating clerical jobs even though I have wanted to leave. I will continue to call upon Lilith to push me out there, doing what I want to do, stepping to the front of the stage, and showing who I am."

"Inspired by Lilith, I have abstained from sexual relationships for four years by giving priority to my independence. My life has improved on all levels. I have slowed down and am learning to have a relationship with myself. My friendships are deeper. My relationship with money has improved. I am less preoccupied with obsessions. All in all, I feel that my life is manageable and full. In the past, I was either swirling over my previous relationship or looking for someone new. For brief periods I would do some positive things for myself, but I always had one eye out for the next distraction."

*Laura's Poem in Praise of Lilith and Eve:*
> In praise of the hard and the soft within myself, within all women.
> In praise of the rigor, honesty, and strength that cracked the armor.
> In praise of the powerful thrust from within, saying:
>> *Birth yourself, Laura—that is your imperative.*
>> *Be soft again only when you are willing to be whole.*
> In praise of the strength and austerity of my intelligence
>> and its refusal to compromise with lies.
> In praise of healing reversals that speak the whole truth,
>> and nothing but the truth—it is right and good that I am a woman.

---

"Neuroscience shows that more than 1 million new neural connections are formed every second in the first three years of life. Relationships with a child's primary caregivers directly affect the type and quality of these connections. Caring and connected parent/child relationships are major factors in shaping how we relate to the world, including our capacity to empathize, learn, imagine, and create. The quality of parenting we support as a society also directly affects our economy and our democracy. —Riane Eisler, CenterforPartnership.org

---

## A Pause Between Chapters
### *Mary's Many Names*

Mary is known by many names. I was given the book "Key of Heaven" as a young girl at St. Joseph's Village. I read the list of her names often, feeling her soothing "mother" presence and her powerful "queen" presence in the words as I recited the list.

Later, I came to understand that Mary was central to the Catholic Church's marketing campaign. Unlike the Protestants, the Catholics had an accessible female god, fashioned after the Goddess, who was worshipped by the masses. Mary became the people's god. Most Catholic women, including my grandmother, prayed to Mary rather than to the invisible and usually angry father god or the bloody Jesus on the cross featured in most Catholic churches.

Imagine reading this list of names and seeing pictures and statues of the Queen of Heaven daily as a young girl. Imagine this young girl becoming a teenager and being filled with confusion and shame by the very names and images that comforted her throughout childhood.

Holy Mary
Holy Mother of God
Holy Virgin of Virgins

Mother of Christ
Mother of the Church
Mother of Divine Grace
Mother most Pure
Mother most Chaste
Mother Inviolate
Mother Undefiled
Mother most Amiable
Mother most Admirable
Mother of Good Counsel
Mother of our Creator
Mother of our Savior

Virgin most Prudent
Virgin most Venerable
Virgin most Renowned

Virgin most Powerful
Virgin most Merciful
Virgin most Faithful

Mirror of Justice
Seat of Wisdom
Cause of our Joy

Spiritual Vessel
Vessel of Honor
Singular Vessel of Devotion

Mystical Rose
Tower of David
Tower of Ivory
House of Gold
Ark of the Covenant
Gate of Heaven
Morning Star
Health of the Sick

Refuge of Sinners
Comforter of the Afflicted
Help of Christians

Queen of Heaven
Queen of Angels
Queen of Patriarchs
Queen of Prophets
Queen of Apostles
Queen of Martyrs
Queen of Confessors
Queen of Virgins
Queen of All Saints
Queen of Families
Queen of Peace
Queen of the Holy Rosary
Queen Assumed into Heaven

# CHAPTER 7

## An Encounter with Mary
### The Mother of Jesus

*"Women have to suspect that the entire symbolic universe that surrounds them, which has socialized them to their roles, is deeply tainted by hostility to their humanity. Once that is clear, the very grammar they have been taught to use to express themselves and the symbols they use to praise God become bitter-tasting." —Rosemary Radford Ruether, Sexism and God-Talk*

*"The reason for the continuing effects of religious symbols is that the mind is uncomfortable with a vacuum. Symbol systems cannot simply be rejected, they must be replaced. Where there is no replacement, the mind will revert to familiar structures at times of crisis, bafflement, or defeat." —Carol Christ, WomanSpirit Rising*

As the face of god changed in my experience, I wondered about Mary. My own memories of her were confusing. She had been both elevated and demeaned. In the Catholic orphanage of my elementary school years, she was presented as the Queen of Heaven. In the Catholic Missal I was given there was a 'Litany to the Blessed Virgin Mary' that listed 48 names for her, including twelve concerning her queenship. The pictures of her I kept in my Missal were queenly indeed. She was high and lofty, and surrounded by stars and halos, crowns and crescent moons.

In the Protestant church of my adolescence, there were no statues of Mary, no Missals with pictures of the Queen of Heaven, no feasts in honor of the Blessed Virgin, no rosaries or Hail Marys. Mary was mentioned only once a year church-school plays in which she was portrayed as a meek adolescent with a pregnant belly, covered head, and downcast eyes. The Protestants had dethroned Mary and I had to go into hiding with my love and devotion to her.

Mary's journey from heaven where she reigned as honored Queen to earth where she was reduced to obedient handmaiden, was orchestrated by men. Would it be possible to disentangle her story from the all-encompassing salvation drama of the father who sent his son to earth by way of Mary's womb? Is there a middle space where earth and heaven meet; where the Queen of Heaven, virginal and perfect, meets the Mary of Earth, embodied and human?

## Mary and Eve: Contrasting Visions
Although the gods of Judaism and Christianity allow no woman to share his power or throne, Mary is the one sacred female who has come the closest to storming his heavens. She's maintained a stubborn presence within religious discussion, devotional literature, classical art, and within the hearts of her followers and the anger of her detractors throughout the centuries.

Mary appears often in the writings of women. She is remembered with a mixture of awe, anger, and confusion. Many women spend their lives either emulating or rejecting the image of her presented in the churches of their childhoods. As we acknowledged earlier in the book, most women cannot imagine the divine as woman because of the negative and often confusing portrayal of religious women through word, image, and story in our childhood churches. Like Eve and Lilith, Mary was presented to us through the eyes of men. Catholics and Protestants were offered contrasting visions of her.

The Protestant Mary was confined to earth. She was only valued for the role she played in Jesus' birth. We are not given many details of her life in the Scriptural record, only those facts most pertinent to her role as mother of Jesus. Her story revolves around the men in her life—Joseph, her husband; Jesus, her son; and the Lord God, her Master in heaven. She lived in a culture in which women were legally the possessions of men. Before Mary's marriage, she was under her father's authority. At her marriage, she became the property of Joseph. And when Joseph died, a disciple of Jesus was appointed to care for her. Mary was a good and faithful adolescent Jewish girl who obeyed the dictates of god and man.

The Catholics, on the other hand, raised Mary above life with lofty words about her virginity (Holy Virgin of Virgins), and her immaculate conception (Queen Conceived Without Sin). In catechism classes and weekly sermons, there were only a few references to the human dimensions of her life as the wife of Joseph and the mother of Jesus. Rather, it was her participation in the elaborate drama of human salvation reaching back to Eve that was of utmost importance. The unfolding of this salvation drama in the misogynistic imagination, thinking, and writing of the church fathers and theologians inextricably linked the stories of Mary and Eve. In a tragic sense, they have been rivals throughout religious history. Their existence was fashioned in reaction and response to the other—by men.

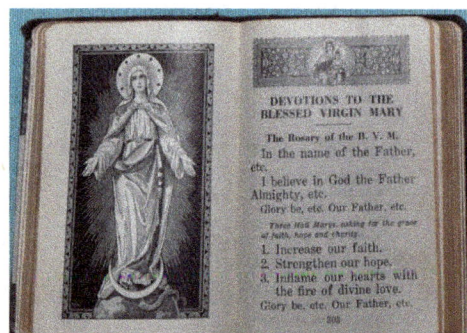

> Eve is the Mother of Evil, who was disobedient and sexually sinful. Humanity's fall from grace was instigated by the loss of her innocence and virginity.
>> Mary is the Mother of Good, who was obedient and virginal. Humanity's salvation through grace was transacted through her virgin body.

> Eve elevated disobedience. By eating the fruit, Eve disobeyed God's command and released sin, misery, and death into the human experience.
>> Mary elevated obedience. Through her obedience, the savior entered the world. She obeyed God's command with these words: "Do unto me according to your will.'

Eve elevated sexuality. She committed the sexual act. Her body seduced the good man Adam to join her in sin. She was exiled from the heavens as Whore.

> Temptress Mary elevated virginity. She abstains forever from the sexual act. Her body is eternally covered and beyond desire. She is allowed in heaven as Madonna and Virgin of Virgin.

Eve is the Fallen Mother. She experienced suffering in childbirth. She bore children in pain.

> Mary is the Sacred Mother. She experienced joy, not pain in childbirth.

Eve is the Human Mother. God gave birth to her.

> Mary is the Heavenly Mother. She gave birth to God.

As children, we weren't aware of the elaborate theological discussions concerning Mary except as they took up residence within us by way of repetitive songs, prayers, and religious scenes. The Mass itself was a captivating sacred drama. It mesmerized us as it was indoctrinating us. In Mythic Mother circles, women share their remembrances of Mary. Add your story to theirs.

> "Mary was a non-person with no anger and no spine. She was the only female I saw in church, and she was only half human, reduced as she was to only good qualities. This irked my mother and she rejected the church in part because of it."

> "In the front of the church there was a crucifix with Jesus on it and over to the right, not quite as prominently positioned, was a statue of Mary. That was confusing. Was she equal to god or not? Was I expected to live up to this ideal woman? I remember very distinctly saying the rosary to her. I can feel this memory in my fingers."

> "To us Protestants, Mary was an object, an empty vessel, a space holder for the divine Christ. She was insignificant. I remember my mom explaining that 'those Catholics' worshipped Mary and how ridiculous that was. I got the impression that "those Catholics" were frivolous and wasting their time praying to "just" a woman."

## Marketing Mary

Mary was expelled from the Bible after she performed her duty as the passive channel through which father god sent his only begotten son to earth. Her experience was not valued, nor did it become part of the orthodox record of the early Church. Nevertheless, Mary did re-emerge as a powerful force throughout history. As Christianity spread through Europe, it had to reckon with the Mother Goddess. Because she was so deeply rooted in people's lives and consciousness the Church fathers eventually realized they were powerless to eliminate her. The Christianity they offered was unappealing because its god was male with no female icons comparable to the Goddess. Mary changed all that.

Although Mary was expelled from the Biblical text, she was not forgotten by women. They would not let her memory die. Stories about her circulated among the people and mingled with stories of the Goddess. To women, Mary became the manifestation of the Goddess. She became the accessible One who looked like them and who felt, cried, and understood them because she was a woman. Women have always needed to relate to a god who looks like them.

In order to gain converts, the church fathers capitalized on the melding of these two images. Just as the rabbis demoted the Goddess to fit within their misogynistic creation myths, so too the Church fathers swallowed the Goddess, Queen of Heaven and Earth, into their unfolding theology as the Virgin Mary. Layered atop the meager details we have of Mary's life are centuries of imaginative renderings in which she was reconstructed as the Queen of Heaven.

To appease followers of the Goddess, the Church Fathers wove some of the Goddess' qualities into the image of Mary. At the same time, they eliminated those qualities they found disturbing to their worldview. Mary was stripped of the Goddess' willfulness, independence, and sexual freedom. To domesticate the Goddess made perfect sense from the male perspective. However, from a woman's perspective, it was a tragic choice, one that presented generations of girl-children with a distorted image of womanhood in which passivity, chastity, and domestication became the primary feminine ideals to cultivate in girls and women.

Over time, the Queen of Heaven developed a life of her own among the people. She was the Goddess reborn. She refused to stay in her place as defined by the Church fathers. She refused to allow them to dictate the terms of her existence. The people worshipped Her as the Goddess. The Church fathers attempted to contain her. But eventually they recognized that the worship of the Goddess, reincarnated as the Queen of Heaven, could not be stopped so they swallowed her festivals, beliefs, and images into their developing theologies. And they transformed ancient Goddess shrines into the chapels of the Queen of Heaven.

### Reversals of Value

In graduate school I read a Kierkegaardian parable that reminds me of the poignant reversals of adolescence. It has followed me, finding its way from one journal to the next:

> Late at night thieves entered a store and did their work without detection. In the morning it was obvious to the clerk that the store had been entered, yet nothing seemed to have been taken. As customers brought merchandise to the counter, the clerk noticed a curious phenomenon—the merchandise of least value wore the tags of greatest value and the items of greatest value carried the tags of least value. By the end of the day the puzzle was solved: the thieves had taken nothing—instead they reversed the price tags."

Patriarchy reverses the tags in a conformity-based childhood. The natural and essential self, a priceless treasure, is criticized and set aside, and the artificial, constructed self grows in value.

Image is more valuable than essence; conformity, more priceless than originality; coloring inside the lines, more acceptable than spontaneity. At a certain age we are expected to move beyond "childish" ways and settle into what Rachel Carson described as the "boredom and the disenchantments of later years, the sterile preoccupation with things that are artificial, the alienation from the sources of our strength."

And as we reviewed in Chapter 5, Madonna Kolbenschlag *(Kiss Sleeping Beauty Good-Bye)* summed up Season 2 in this way, "At seventeen the young woman is well on her way to being a formula female." For Catholics, the church used their version of Mary (in concert with their version of Eve) to reverse the tags, robbing us of our exquisite internal sources of strength, willfulness, and embodiment.

### A Reversal of Value: Our Willfulness

*In the beginning, as defined by men, Eve asserted her will against god. She refused to obey and ate the fruit. This was the ultimate evil that plunged all of humankind into sin. She was cursed and exiled from the garden of life. Eve's predecessor, Lilith, embodied rebelliousness. She refused to submit to god or man. Her exertive willfulness was labeled evil and unfeminine. She was exiled from the Bible as the rebellious first woman.*

*In the beginning of Christian history, the earthly Mary was shaped and molded by men to eliminate a woman's capacity for choice and independent action. Without any resistance, she allowed her body and reputation to be disrupted. She allowed others to shape her life, destiny, and choices. She was the willing vessel and container for the birth of Christ. She surrendered to god's will.*

At every point in religious history, our willfulness was assaulted. The image of Mary was shaped according to men's specifications in order to convince us that we are incapable of independent thought and action, of self-determining choice, of the successful implementation of our desires in the world, and of controlling our own lives and destinies. As children we were taught to emulate Mary. She was kind and loving; we were to be kind and loving. She surrendered to god's will; we were to surrender to god's will. She was blessed because she obeyed; we would be blessed if we obeyed.

Convinced that our lives are not our own, we become alienated from our inner sense of what is right and appropriate for us. We spend our lifetimes trying to fit into someone else's idea of what is right for us. We assemble our bodies according to society's formula of the perfect woman. We form our thoughts and opinions to suit the audience. We limit our feelings to what's acceptable. We formulate our behaviors and actions according to the expectations of others. Some of us are emotionally crippled as a result of habitually abandoning ourselves. Our true form, in danger of dissolving as each surrender becomes a mini-abdication of who we are.

*In the beginning, as defined by men, Eve elevated sexuality. She committed the sexual act. Her body seduced Adam to join her in sin. As a result, she was exiled from heaven as Whore and Temptress. Eve's predecessor, Lilith embodied assertive sexuality. She refused to submit to the man, to lie beneath him. Her unfettered sexuality was her fatal flaw. She is exiled from the Bible as Demon Mother and Tormentor of Men.*

*In the beginning of Christian history, the Queen of Heaven was shaped by men to eliminate the woman's body and its troublesome sexuality. The Sacred Woman elevates virginity; she abstains forever from the sexual act. Her body is eternally covered and beyond desire. The Virgin Mary was robbed of her body and stripped of her sexuality. She is allowed in the heavens only as Madonna and Virgin of all Virgins.*

At every point in religious history, women's bodies have been assaulted by male priests, ministers, rabbis, theologians, and religious writers. Men have always feared women's bodies. Religious males in particular have had a powerful obsession with them. They have written volumes on the subject. Instead of dealing with their own attitudes, their own sexuality, and their own responses to our bodies, they have twisted us out of shape through their teachings and theologies. Our bodies bear the brunt of their deeply embedded fear of the feminine.

As we read in Chapters 3 and 5, the maleness of god and the inferiority of women were woven into the religious literature, instruction, and ritual that surrounded us in childhood. According to Aristotle's biology, the male form is normative and when distorted by female matter, it produced an inferior species—woman. Thomas Aquinas also considered the male the normative sex of the human species. He believed that the male represented the fullness of human nature, whereas woman is defective physically, morally, and mentally.

When humankind's salvation required that the heavenly god 'become flesh and dwell among us,' the church fathers sought to eliminate any possibility that the baby Jesus would be defiled on his passage through a female body. Their solution was to eliminate her womb altogether. They referred to the place of Christ's gestation as a 'casket.' In the words of a male theologian, "Christ is the gleaming jewel contained in the casket which is Mary." The term 'casket' conjures up images of a mini coffin or container with satin-covered walls. Its misogynistic purpose was to protect "the son of god" from the defilement of entering life through a woman's messy, bloody, and inferior body. By using the casket image, men once again denied a woman's intimate involvement in the origins of life.

After her task was completed, Mary was transformed into the Queen of Heaven. She was allowed into the kingdom of god as the eternal virgin with an unbroken hymen and as the sacred mother of the savior son. As virgin and mother, Mary served as an unreachable ideal for good girls who desired to emulate her. How could we be mother, requiring the sexual act, and at the same time, virgin with an unbroken hymen? Our bodies—along with their natural desires and sexual inclinations—were twisted out of shape and labeled evil by a religion that preferred men and worshipped a male god.

*Flipping the Tags: Reclaiming our Willfulness and our Bodies*
The first step toward the truth is consulting women's history, reaching back to a time before god the father was imagined into being. A time when ancient women refused to surrender except to the natural rhythms of life, when virginity meant a woman was "one in herself," owned by no man, author of her own life, creator of her own destiny. YES, there it is again, a return to the very beginning flips the misogynistic text back around again to the truth. The words of Marija Gimbutas and Nor Hall informed my personal reclamation project:

> "The Goddess of the Paleolithic and Neolithic is parthenogenetic, creating life out of herself. She is a primeval, self-fertilizing virgin Goddess. The Christian virgin is a demoted version of this virginal deity." —Marija Gimbutas, *Civilization of the Goddess*

> "Virgin means One in Herself; not maiden inviolate, but maiden alone, in herself. To be virginal does not mean to be chaste, but rather to be true to nature and instinct." —Nor Hall, *The Moon and the Virgin*

In our circles, we renamed the Mythic Mary—SHE WHO IS COMPLETE IN HERSELF. As we glimpsed HER face, we turned around—instead of looking outside of ourselves for salvation, we turned toward our own inner resources. We returned home to the very beginning when we embodied willfulness, creative energy, deep wisdom, and resilient body-love. We re-membered that in the very beginning we loved ourselves and that in the *very* beginning of human history, our Mythic Mothers were powerful Goddesses! We invited SHE WHO IS COMPLETE IN HERSELF to visit our circles. Her words became part of our evolving Book of Woman.

## An Encounter with Mary
*I am Mary, the Willful Goddess.*
I stride the earth in willfulness.
I am She Who is Complete in Herself.
My life is my own. I belong to no man.
I am the author of my life.
I am the creatress of my own destiny.

> Take back your life. Connect with your virgin-self, the whole and complete center within you. Value your will. Know your will and believe it is valid and achievable in the world. Assert your will in harmony with your deeper wisdom.

Be self-determined. Do not allow others to dictate the terms of your existence or your belief. Design your own life. Name your own gods. Honor all that has been demeaned. Receive all that has been cast aside. Your willfulness is good. It is very good.

### I am Mary, the Source of Life.

I stride the earth in fruitfulness.
My watery womb is the fertile birthplace of all that is:
the dark abyss that swallows the Sun God each evening;
the chalice from which you drink your wine in sacred ceremonies.
Out of the moist darkness of my womb, new images are born.

In your creativity, you are one with me and free to choose your own form of birthing. Each child, a new expression of creative energy, brought into the world by the Mother. Each poem and painting, ritual and ceremony, inspiring a new vision, reflecting the field of infinite possibility offered to the world by its creator—you!

Blessed are the creative fruits of your womb, springing forth in new images and new life. Honor all that has been demeaned. Receive all that has been cast aside. The creative womb is good. It is very good.

### I am Mary, True to Nature and Instinct

I reach toward Wisdom's depths.
to remind you that all you need is found there.

Blessed be the wisdom within you that orchestrated your movements from crawling to walking to running; your sounds from garbles to words to sentences; and your knowing of the world through your amazing senses.

The flow of wisdom has been faithful to call you home to yourself even when you have detoured from what was healthy and good. Wisdom's graceful, fluid presence lives in and through you, and unfolds in synch with your truest self.

### I am Mary, the Virgin Goddess.

I stride the earth in nakedness.
No robes hide the beauty of my fertile vulva,
my rounded belly, and my full breasts.
I am She Who is Complete in Herself.

I live in my body. I embrace its desires as my own.
Allow your acquaintance with me to transform
your relationship to your body.

*Your body is your own.* Live in your body. Trusts its natural instincts. Connect with your virgin self, the whole and complete center within you. Choose to be alone, to reunite with yourself, to touch a long-lost part of you, to hold your body with tenderness and with passion. Embark on an intimate journey with yourself. Experience fullness, self-possession, and satisfaction. Delight in your freedom to be alone, to meet your own needs, and to give yourself pleasure.

*Your body is your own.* Feel the fire rise within you. Learn of its ways, its awakening, its path to union. Celebrate your body-sensations. They are calling you to your edges. Imagine a marriage within you. Lover uncoiling to meet lover. Height calling to depth. Earth moving toward heaven. A middle space within you.

What will you learn from this journey into the depths of you? Will you no longer need a lover? The Goddesses loved themselves to their edges. Self-possessed, they strode the earth. This my prayer for you, blessed woman: *Rise, fire, rise. Uncoil within her. Rise from her depths. Awaken each center. Unite with her spirit. May joy will be the fruit of her union.*

> Honor all that has been demeaned.
> Receive all that has been cast aside.
> Your body is good. It is very good.

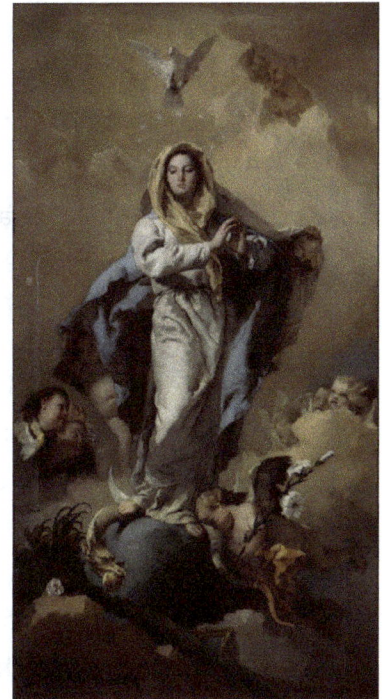

## The Protestant Mary and Catholic Mary Meet

Reminded of Madonna Kolbenschlag's words that we do not change because of "intellectual convictions or ethical inclinations, but rather through transformed imaginations," I wrote the poem "Contrasting Visions." As part of my own reclaiming journey, I imagined into being the untold stories of the virginal Catholic Mary and the obedient Protestant Mary.

*The Catholic Mary*
I could not see the Queen of Heaven's body
through her clothes.
I wonder, what was she hiding
beneath those floor length robes:
her breasts and pubic hair?

Perhaps the Queen of Heaven has no body
like the paintings and statues fashioned in her image,

were her robes painted atop a blank canvas
or chiseled into an absent body?

The Queen of Heaven was stripped of her earthiness.
She answered my prayers
yet she could not tell me how it felt
to join my body with another.
What else could one expect?
She lived in the heavens with the men
a neuter, untouchable and untouched.

### The Protestant Mary

The Sunday School Mary had a body,
a young woman's soft and lovely body.
Overshadowed by the power of the Most High,
no loving arms attended her opening.
The pregnant Mary,
her belly and breasts growing in fullness,
spilling over with the life of god.

The Mary of Earth had a body, yet it wasn't hers,
god could do whatever he wanted to it.
Stripped of her will, kept in her place,
quietly surrendering to those who know best,
she accepted her role as mother,
only a mother, to the exclusion of all else,
to the denial of her own life.
Where was her voice?
Did she ever say, "No More"?

### All Is Not as It Seems

I imagine the Mary of Earth confused, troubled, and angry
within the secrecy of her heart, where no man could hear her.
Mary, reclaiming her will, daring to question
the outrageous, the disruptive, and the inhumane.
Mary, reclaiming her voice, shouting, "No More."

If the Mary of Earth discovered a place to assert her will
to question the dictates of gods and men,
I wonder, did the Queen of Heaven

have a place to own her body? Did she masturbate?

Was her place of rebellion in the darkness of the night
where she could not be reached by definitions
imposed by priests and kings?
Was her bed a virgin bed in which she nightly
shed her robes and savored her woman-body,
"This is my body. I will take and eat."

### Carol's Story: Thank you, Mom

"In praise of my mother who allowed me freedom from the Church. She didn't have a spirituality of her own, but she did have a basically woman-affirming perspective on life. This led her to be deeply suspicious of the Church and its priests.

"She was openly resentful of the Church's views on marriage and child rearing. She rejected the feminine stereotypes that were forced on her. She was a deeply sensual person, and she felt oppressed by the social rigidity of the Church.

"Her independence of the Church's influence allowed me to take all of it—Mass, catechism, priests, nuns, my father in his religious persona, and God Himself, with a grain of salt. Even though we went through the motions to avoid incurring my father's wrath, it was clear that she did not swallow what the Church was handing out, and that I didn't have too either."

### In Memoriam: Marcelline Niemann

At the age of 18, Marcelline joined the Sisters of Charity, committing her life to education. After 25 years of service, she left the BVM community to continue a life dedicated to helping others through education, spiritual guidance, working for social justice, healing the planet and supporting incarcerated men and women, especially those on death row. She wrote the poem *Death/Resurrection* after an encounter with Mother God.

### Death/Resurrection
Yards and yards
Of heavy black serge
Covered every inch of me
Save face and hands
Not a curve
Not a limb
Not a hint
Of my beautiful
Woman-body
Could be seen.

No wind
Could blow through my hair
Swirl my skirts
Playfully
Around my thighs.
Warm moist earth
Never tickled
My firmly-shod feet.

Thus was I bound
Bride of Christ.
For twenty-five youthful years,
The male magisterium
Male theologians
Male spiritual directors
Properly dressed
My body
And my soul.

Then God the Mother
Released me

I, Sensual woman
Earthy woman
Beautiful woman
Am good.

"In the beginning, people prayed to the Creatress of Life, the Mistress of Heaven.
At the very dawn of religion, God was a woman. Do you remember?"
Merlin Stone, *When God Was a Woman*

# CHAPTER 8

## *Reclaiming Our Original Spirituality*

*"We must choose our own kneeling places and
not have thrust upon us an agenda foreign to our spirits."*
Marilyn Sewell, Cries of the Spirit

In the very beginning of her life, the girl-child has direct access to the spirit of life. It is as near to her as the breath that fills her. And it connects her to everything. She is not alone. Her spirit is one with the spirit of her beloved grandmother, her favorite rock, tree, and star. She develops her own methods for contacting the spirit in all things.

She climbs a tree and sits in its branches, listening. She loves the woods and listens there too. She has a special friend—a rock. She gives it a name and eats her lunch with it whenever she can. She keeps the window open next to her bed even on the coldest of nights. She loves the fresh air on her face. She pulls the covers tight around her chin and listens to the mysterious night sky. She believes that her grandmother is present even though everyone else says she is dead. Each night, she drapes the curtain over her shoulders for privacy, looks out the window near her bed, listens for Grandma and then says silent prayers to her.

Her imagination is free for a time. She does not need priest or teacher to describe god to her. Spirit erupts spontaneously in colorful and unique expressions. God is Grandma, the twinkling evening star, the gentle breeze that washes across her face, the peaceful quiet darkness after everyone has fallen asleep, and all the colors of the rainbow. The spirit of the universe pulsates through her. She is full of herself.

Eventually the girl-child will turn away from the Spirit-filled One. Her original spirituality will become confined within the acceptable lines of religion. She will be taught the "correct" way to name and imagine god. As we explored in Chapter 4, he will be mediated to her by way of the words, images, stories, and myths shaped, written, and spoken by men. She will adopt the god she is given. It is too dangerous to rebel. If she dares to venture out of the lines by communing with the spirit of a tree, the mysterious night sky, or her grandma, she will be labeled heretic, backslider, or witch. She is told:

> Prideful One, your grandma is not god; neither is your favorite star or rock. God has only one name and face. You shall have no gods before him. God is Father, Son, and Holy Ghost. He is found in the church, heavens, and holy book, not in you. God is the god of the fathers and sons; the daughters have no say in the matter.

The Spirit-Filled One falls asleep. Occasionally she awakens to remind the girl-child-turned-woman of what she once knew. These periodic reminders are painful. The woman fills her life with distractions so she will not hear the quiet inner voice, calling her to return home. Years later, new teachers enter the woman's life—a therapist, a self-help group, a support circle, a beloved friend, or perhaps this book. They remind her of what she once knew:

> Spirit-filled One, your grandma is god and so are your favorite star and rock. God has many names and many faces. God is Mother, Daughter, and Wise Old Crone. She is found in your mothers, your daughters, and in you. She is Mother of all Living and blessed are her daughters. You are girl-woman made in her image. The spirit of the universe pulsates through you.

## Empowering Resistance

### Reclaiming the truth of our beginnings . . .

<u>With Eve</u>, we reject the dominance of a creation myth that portrays women as the instigators of evil and that excludes the Mother from the creation of the world. We reject the shame-based messages of family, religion, and society that stressed our wrongs, defects, and insufficiencies. We embrace a woman-affirming spirituality that celebrates the Mother's intimate involvement in the origins of life and reminds us of our original goodness.

<u>With Lilith</u>, we reject the dominance of religious myths that exiled strong women and portrayed us as powerless victims. We reject the shame-based messages of family, religion, and society that emphasized our inability to function independently in our own lives. We embrace a woman-affirming spirituality that reminds us of our original power, courage, and independence.

<u>With Mary</u>, we reject the dominance of religious myths and theologies that exiled willful and sexually autonomous women. We reject the shame-based messages of family, religion, and society that require the surrender of our bodies and wills to the dictates of others. We embrace a woman-affirming spirituality that affirms our autonomy, willfulness, and erotic potential.

### Reclaiming our self-sovereignty . . .

We reclaim our self-sovereignty and boldly name our own gods. Beginning in the metaphorical Garden of Eden where Adam named the animals and the woman, 'owning' has been the prerogative of men. Women were not encouraged to name god or to define spirituality. To name the god of our understanding as goddess or woman god, and to speak her name aloud requires monumental courage in a world dominated by male-centered religions.

Courageous women, however, are reclaiming the divine feminine today. Surrounded by women from every age and inspired by Eve, Lilith, and Mary's courage, women are committing the forbidden acts of naming and imagining the god of their understanding as Mother Goddess. Although we are not all devotees of the goddess, it was essential for us to extend our historical and theological vision to include the divine feminine.

Some find HER within traditional religion in the images and stories of Eve, Lilith, and Mary, Sophia and Shekinah, Miriam and Esther, Naomi and Ruth, Tamar and Susanna, and countless unnamed women. They are incorporating these women's stories into their liturgies and prayers. Others find HER on the margins of patriarchal history in the images and stories of the Goddess. They're incorporating her images into their paintings and songs, altars and prayers, and they're weaving HER ancient festivals and beliefs into their unfolding spirituality.

Inspired by a view of history that reaches beyond the beginning defined by men, women are now claiming theological equality with religious traditions and reclaiming the richness of their own imaginations. No longer held hostage by a truncated view of history or by the dominance of the Genesis account of creation, our imaginations are once again free.

I used my imagination to rewrite the familiar prayers and songs of childhood, like the "Hail Mary" and "Our Father" prayers to counteract the father-centered rituals, readings, and beliefs that permeated my childhood. For both prayers, I used the unique rhythm and cadence imprinted upon my memory from years of saying those prayers. I re-wrote them from a non-hierarchical perspective, acknowledging the spirit of life within us, not hovering above us.

The "Hail Mary" as written:
Hail Mary, full of grace, the Lord is with thee. Blessed art thou among women, and blessed is the fruit of thy womb, Jesus. Holy Mary, Mother of God, pray for us sinners now and at the hour of our death. Amen. (The Catholic Daily Missal)
As re-written: "Hail Mary, full of grace, we are one with you. Blessed are you among all living. And blessed are the creative fruits of your Virginity, springing forth in new images and new life. Holy Mary, Mother Goddess, from your breasts flow fountains of living water. From your maternal deep, we are born again unto self-love and self-celebration. With your womb-waters, bless the fertile ground of our creativity.

The "Our Father" as written:
Our Father, who art in heaven, hallowed be thy name. Thy kingdom come, thy will be done, on earth as it is in heaven. Give us this day our daily bread and forgive us our trespasses as we forgive those who trespass against us. And lead us not into temptation, but deliver us from evil. For thine is the kingdom, the power, and the glory, forever. Amen
As re-written: "Our Mother who art within us, we celebrate your many names. Your wisdom come, your love far flung, unfolding from the depths of us. Each day you give

us what we need. You remind us of our limits and we let go. You support us in our power and we act with courage. For you are the dwelling place within us, the empowerment around us, and the celebration among us. As it was in the very beginning, may it be now."

For some women designing a self-defined spirituality centered on "Mother Goddess" does not work. Their journey through the material in this book, and others like it, is motivated by an intellectual curiosity. They have no desire to replace a male god with a female goddess even though they understand the historic significance of the Goddess. For others, painful childhood experiences inflicted by their own mothers make it impossible for them to envision the divine as a loving mother.

Instead, many of these women embrace the natural world as their inspiration. They remember their childhood experiences in nature and their intuitive connection to its rhythms and cycles. Their spirituality reflects the lessons they learned from nature's mystery, beauty, and strength, and from their ongoing connection to its rhythms and cycles. Here is how one circle member described her connection to the natural world:

> "My love of nature has helped me recognize the face of the Earthy Goddess. I call on Her roaring waters when I need strength; on the brightness of the sun, when I am afraid; and on Her gentle breeze to calm me. By becoming one with nature, I embrace my pain and feel it as part of the world's pain. I embrace my power and experience it as the life force flowing through me. I accept myself just as I am, part of it all: the cycles, the harmony, and the rhythm of the natural world from which I came and to which I will return someday."

Others embrace a scientific viewpoint that includes our evolution as a species. Many of these women leave religion altogether and discover that ordinary life is interesting and inspiring enough for them. They find sanctuary in the garden and forest, inspiration in the awesomeness of the night sky, communities of meaning at the local homeless shelter, and rituals of gratitude in shared meals and experiences. Having released their belief in religion's afterlife, they participate fully in life here and now!

In circles of transformation, women support each other to release the conformity of a lifetime by naming their own gods and articulating their own beliefs. Allow their courage to inspire you to write your own "This I Believe" declaration. As we have experienced throughout this book, it matters what we believe.

### This I Believe

> "I now pray to Mother God every morning. She is transforming my experience of being a woman. Surprisingly, I have even thanked her for making me a woman."

"My deepening relationship with the divine feminine has altered my entire cosmology, including how I view myself, other women, the world I live in, the options available to me, and my awareness and understanding of my own personal history. Reclaiming Eve's former glory as the Mother of All Living has been one the most freeing experience of my life."

"I have come to believe that intuition is my emotional and spiritual guide. When I need a less abstract image than intuition, I visualize a tender painting on an old holy water holder of Mary holding Jesus. It was given to me by my aunt before she died. This image helps me see my intuition as a tender, nurturing mother, who holds and supports me. And it links my childhood Catholicism with my adult spirituality."

"I affirm that my spirituality will arise from within me. As it takes shape, I will look for a spiritual community that closely reflects my beliefs and experience. I can struggle no longer, thinking something is wrong with me because I do not fit into another's belief system and god. I have a right to name the god of my understanding, not as the ultimate Truth, but as the truth that is spoken within my own life."

"By dismantling the EVE-story I learned in my childhood church, I have stopped asking the question "what's wrong with me" The running commentary of judgment had been background noise, like "Talk Radio" in the head, going on all the time, and rarely pausing. I have changed this station. I am now living in "what's right with me," in my own present, in this fine moment. I honor, respect, and love the outrageous woman I am. I will put my own loving arms around myself, today and every day. Thank you, EVE!"

"I have begun to use the term Goddess for the first time. This name has amplified as it has reverberated from within, growing from a soft, ashamed whisper to a vigorous and not-to-be denied expression. I have begun to soften my self-criticism and self-rejection in Her name. When I feel the tendency to brutalize myself, I imagine the loving presence of a gentle figure—not the half-conscious austere and phallic one born of our culture, but the one who is tender and full of sympathy. Her movement is one of recognition and connection."

"Since my rejection of religion, I've ached for a spiritual path that would satisfy me. I longed to feel closer to 'god,' but needed a religion that supported my equality to men. I explored Buddhism and Hinduism. I practiced yoga and meditation. These paths felt better to me than my childhood religion, but they still didn't fit. I then stumbled onto the Goddess, who was worshipped before the god of Jehovah killed her worshippers and confiscated her land. I met women honoring the Goddess today, treating the earth as sacred, and feeling joyful in their bodies. I have finally found my way to a spirituality that fits. I now pray to the Goddess, but do not bow my head in shame. I pray with my head upturned and my feet planted on the ground."

"One evening, after reading about the Goddesses and ancient religion's celebration of the whole of a woman, her genitals and sexuality, her anger and wrath, and her power, I had a remarkable experience with my husband. As we were making love, the images of the stone Goddesses kept rising up in front of me. I felt as much in my body as I've ever been in my life. I felt that every inch of me was beautiful and that there was nothing to be loathed or shamed. Something in me was healed that day. The god of my childhood didn't have sexuality, sensuality, passion, music, or colors so I concluded that all these things in me were superfluous and should be dried up. Now I realize these are my essence as a woman."

"The 'Celebrating the Girl-Child' song of welcome touched me. The thought that I deserve lovingkindness, safety, and laughter every day of my life is a liberating concept. In the few seconds it took me to read those words, I was freed from the layers of shame that have kept me from believing that I am worthy to receive good things in my life. You mean I actually deserve my two wonderfully beautiful children? Yes! Yes! And as I reflect on their lovely faces when I read: 'Look at her closely. There is no blemish. She is a delight to behold,' I realize that I am without blemish too. In fact, I'm perfect. It was a deeply healing moment."

"I was uncomfortable hearing Patricia's reworking of the seven days of creation, featuring the Mother instead of the father. The simple act of listening to it felt dangerous to me. I was puzzled by my intense emotion. Words and warnings about heresy and blasphemy paraded through my mind: 'Thou shalt have no other gods before me.' When the feelings of fear and discomfort dissipated, I reread the story to myself. I was able to distance myself from those childhood warnings and acknowledge that the simple story made intuitive sense—that, as Patricia had said, it required less of a leap of faith to imagine the mother giving birth to the world than it did to imagine the father ordering the world into being by a series of verbal commands. That realization was my first step to freedom."

## Woman-Affirming Rituals and Ceremonies

As the face of god changed in my experience, I imagined what it would have been like to experience a weekly gathering that included women and their experience. I rewrote the familiar "liturgy" from a woman's perspective, moving beyond mere pronoun replacement to profound paradigmatic alterations. Over the years, I have gathered many of the re-written bible verses and stories, traditional liturgies and hymns into the below "Imagine" performance piece. Imagine walking into your church, bookstore, or women's center and experiencing the words, images, songs, dances, and affirmations embedded within this performance piece. How might your life have been different?

# An Invocation of WomanSpirit

*Imagine gathering deep in the forest in a circle of women.*
*The priestesses begin with an invocation.*

*We invoke the presence of the Source of All Life.*
Everything in the forest comes from and returns to the Mother. You are as grounded, as connected to Her as the trees are. You are held, supported, and nourished by Her. Acknowledge the firm ground of the Mother holding you.

> *Mother, we welcome you here.*

*We invoke the spirit of life, the breath.*
Everything breathes in the forest. Savor the breath of life, flowing in, through and around you. Inhale deeply as the breath rises from the rich earth beneath you. Release the breath into the cool moist air around you.

> *Breath, we welcome you here.*

*We invoke the wisdom of the body.*
Notice the ancient trees around you. You are one with the forest. Feel your feet grow roots extending deep into the ground. Feel your arms become branches stretching high in the sky. Sway with the breeze. Settle into your woman-body.

> *Wise body, we welcome you here.*

*We invoke the accumulation of our years and experience.*
Notice the forest-dance of life and death and rebirth.
Reach down and touch the forest floor layered with seasons passed.
Look up and view the forest canopy woven from time's evolving.
Acknowledge the seasons of your life. Invoke the richness of your years.

> *Accumulation of years and experience, we welcome you here.*

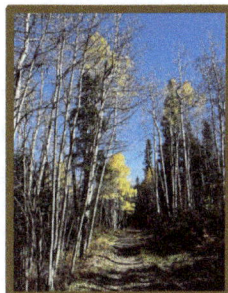

## THE MOTHER OF ALL LIVING
### In The Very Beginning

**Reader:** Imagine hearing stories of an ancient time when it was from the Mother, the giver of life, that the line of the generations was traced; when women were honored for both their capacity to nurture and to accomplish great things; and when virginity meant "woman, complete in herself," owned by no man, creator of her own destiny. Imagine if you heard these words in your childhood home or church. Imagine your children hearing them today.

**Dance and Voice Choir:**

*In the beginning was the Mother.*

On the first day, SHE gave birth to light and darkness.
>   They danced together.

On the second day, SHE gave birth to land and water.
>   They touched.

On the third day, SHE gave birth to green growing things.
>   They rooted and took a deep breath.

On the fourth day, SHE gave birth to land, sea, and air creatures.
>   They walked and flew and swam.

On the fifth day, HER creation learned balance and cooperation.
>   She thanked her partner for coaching her labor.

On the sixth day, SHE celebrated the creativity of all living things.

On the seventh day, SHE left space for the unknown.

**Reader:** Together let us pray:

Our Mother, who art within us, we celebrate your many names. Your wisdom come, your love a constant hum, unfolding from the depths of us. Each day you give us all that we need. You remind us of our limits that we might let go. You support us in our power that we might act with courage. You are the dwelling place within us, the empowerment around us, and the celebration among us. As it was in the very beginning, may it be now.

*"The Mother-Womb, the Creatress of destiny.*
*In pairs she completed them."*
*—Assyrian Scripture*

## THE DIVINE GIRL-CHILD
### A New Birth

Reader: Imagine hearing stories of the Divine Girl-Child whose birth was announced and celebrated by angels, whose coming merited visitors and precious gifts, and in whose honor the peoples of the world gather for a yearly retelling of the story of her birth. Imagine if you heard these words in your childhood home or church. Imagine if your children and grandchildren heard them today.

Dance and Voice Choir

In this hour everything is stillness. There is total silence and awe.
We are overwhelmed with a great wonder. We keep vigil.
We are expecting the coming of the Divine Girl-Child.
In the fullness of time, she is born. She shines like the sun, bright and beautiful.
She is laughing a most joyful laugh. She is a delight, soothing the world with peace.

Become bold. Lean over and look at her. Touch her face.
Lift her in your hands with great awe. There is no blemish on her.
She is splendid to see. She opens her eyes and looks intently at you.

A powerful light comes forth from her eyes, like a flash of lightning. The light of her gaze invites the hidden one to come into the light; the sleeping one to awaken; the frozen one to thaw; the buried one to emerge; and the hard and protected one to soften. Receive her healing gaze deep within your being.

Suddenly there appears a multitude of heavenly beings singing:
"Glory to the Mother of All Living and to her Daughter.
She has arrived. The Divine Child is among us.
She will bring peace and inspire goodwill among all people.

Welcome her joyfully. Shout with a loud voice:
You belong here among us. We're glad you're alive!
Surround her with goodness, safety, and laughter.
She is the Divine Child, come among us this day."

All: For Mother God so loved the world that she sent into its midst the Divine Girl-Child. Whosoever believes in Her goodness, listens to Her wisdom, and celebrates Her power will be awakened to the abundance of gifts within them. (John 3:16, adapted)

*Imagine a world where the girl-child's birth is celebrated with as much pomp, circumstance, and opportunity as her brother's; where her body and natural processes are honored without shame and violence; and where she is allowed equal access to its pulpits and altars, thrones, boardrooms, and negotiating tables. And so it is.*

## THE ONE WHO SHEDS HER BLOOD
### There's Power in The Blood

Reader: Imagine the sacraments and rituals of childhood commemorating the monthly shedding of a woman's blood, her sacred blood that holds within it both life and death. Imagine singing songs and spirituals that celebrate the beautiful, powerful blood of woman. Imagine if you heard these words in your childhood home or church and if your children heard them today.

Voice Choir:
Would you be free from the burden of lies?
> There's power in the blood, power in the blood.
Would you receive deep healing within?
> There's wonderful power in the blood.

Chorus:
There is power, power, wonder-working power
> in the blood of the woman.
There is power, power, wonder-working power
> in the precious blood of the woman.

Voice Choir:
Would you be wiser much wiser than now?
> There's power in the blood, power in the blood.
Shame's stains are lost in her life-giving flow.
> There's wonderful power in the blood.

Chorus:
There is power, power, wonder-working power
> in the blood of the woman.
There is power, power, wonder-working power
> in the precious blood of the woman.

*we need a god who bleeds*
*spreads her lunar vulva & showers us in shades of scarlet*
*thick & warm like the breath of her*
*—Ntsoge Shange*

# THE WISE OLD WOMAN
## Gathering The Years

Reader: Imagine the rituals and sacraments of your childhood church and synagogue presided over by wise old post-menopausal women. In ancient times they were considered the wisest of the wise because they permanently held within them their life-creating wise blood. Imagine if you heard these words in your childhood home or church and if your children heard them today.

## A Circle of Crone Guides

Let us gather our years. Move forward through the years of your life, beginning with your birth. Pay special attention to the years that hurt as you pass through them. Bless the bruised and wounded years. Call out those years.

Now travel again through the years, beginning with your birth. Pay special attention to the years that delight you as you pass through them. Celebrate the bright and comfortable years. Call them out.

Gather all the years of your life in a bundle, the bright and the bruised. Bring that bundle of years into this room. Call out the years you have lived. Fill this sacred space with the accumulation of your years.

Reader 2: Together let us remember,

In the name of the Mother of All Living,
> (Touch your womb center in honor of the mother's intimate connection
> to the origins of life.)

and of the Divine Daughter,
> (Touch your breasts in honor of the daughter's developing body.)

and of the Wise Old Woman,
> (Touch your eyes in honor of the wise inner vision
> acquired through the accumulation of years.)

As it was in the very beginning, may it be now.
> (Open your arms to receive All That Is.)

*"In wisdom, we acknowledge that everything changes.*
*What is born will die. What dies nourishes life in its many forms.*
*We honor the accumulation of our years and our wisdom."*
*The Crone Affirmation*

# The Blessing of our Mythic Mothers

The well was a holy place to our earliest ancestors, a passageway to the underground womb, the maternal deep. While visiting the well, they prayed to the well's resident goddess, asking her to meet their heart's desire. Imagine a well of living water within you.

Gaze into the well and see **EVE**, The Mother of All Living, within you. Her womb waters offer ongoing rebirth and transformation. She looks upon you with mercy and lovingkindness. Her eyes remind you of your original goodness. Reach into the waters as a prayer to The Mother of All Living:

> Source of Life, to you I come,
>
> Welcoming is your womb. Nurturing is your love.
>
> In you, I am enclosed and sustained.
>
> With your womb-waters, bless the fertile ground of my goodness.

Gaze again into the well and see **LILITH**, The Rebellious First Mother. She looks upon you with strength. Her eyes remind you of your original power and courage. From her maternal deep, you are born again unto self-possession and self-respect. Reach into the waters as a prayer to The Rebellious First Mother:

> Source of Life, from you I am pushed.
>
> Strong is your womb. Powerful its thrust.
>
> In you, I exert, initiate, and move.
>
> With your womb-waters, bless the fertile ground of my strength.

Gaze into the well and see **MARY,** the Queen of Heaven, within you. From her breasts flow fountains of living water. Drink of her living water, moistening the ground of creativity within you, calling forth the fruit of your creative womb. Reach into the waters as a prayer to the Queen of Heaven:

> Hail, Mary, full of grace. I am one with you.
>
> Blessed art thou among all living.
>
> And blessed are the creative fruits of your Virginity,
>
> springing forth in new images and new life.
>
> With your womb-waters, bless the fertile ground of my creativity.

Gaze into the well and see **YOUR MOTHER**. She held and nurtured you within her. In the fullness of time, she pushed you from her into your own life, breath, and future. All that she gave birth to is good, you are very good. Across the distance born of anger and love, reach into the waters as a prayer to her:

> Mother, I will free your voice to shout out the pain of a lifetime.
>
> Your silence is mine. My voice is yours.
>
> Your pain is mine. My healing is yours.
>
> Together, we will speak and heal the pain of a lifetime.
>
> With your womb-waters, bless the fertile ground of my wholeness.

*Go from here confident in your goodness, joyful in your creativity,*
*and sustained by your strength. You are blessed by the Mother. And so it is.*

## In Closing: A Warrior's Journey.  A Shared Journey.  An Essential Journey

The journey we have taken to reclaim **EVE** and our Mythic Mothers has been a warrior's journey. We traveled through the critical words, images, experiences, and expectations cluttering our historical, religious, and personal landscapes. The journey called for nothing less than a transformation of our inner worlds, a complete reversal of all we had been taught to believe about ourselves. A mere rearrangement of our outer lives would not do. The journey led us home to ourselves, and to our self-sovereignty.

The journey we have taken to reclaim **EVE** and our Mythic Mothers has been a shared journey. We joined women from every age who have committed the forbidden act of stepping outside systems of thought and belief that denied their very existence. Intellectually, spiritually, and emotionally arrogant women who trust themselves and their own experience. Women who refuse to ask, "What's wrong with me?" Women who make a powerful statement with every thought they share, every feeling they express, and every action they take on their own behalf.

The journey we have taken to reclaim **EVE** and our Mythic Mothers is an essential journey. Our beloved planet is in desperate need of women who are full of themselves. Women who use their personal and communal resources to design woman-affirming solutions to the challenges confronting humankind in the 21st century. Women who give birth to images of inclusion, poems of truth, rituals of healing, experiences of transformation, relationships of equality, strategies of peace, institutions of justice, and households of compassion on behalf of their daughters and sons, and the beloved planet that is our home.

*Thank you for sharing the journey with me.*

> ***Until we imagine something, it remains an impossibility.***
> ***Once imagined, it becomes our experience.***
>
> Imagine a world where the question "what's wrong with me"
> has been exorcised from the bodies and lives of our daughters.
> A world where they cultivate their amazing capacities
> as children of life. Where they travel a less turbulent path
> than we did toward self-love, self-acceptance, and self-trust.
> And so it is.

# Fifty Things to Do

Imagine designing your life without the question "what's wrong with me" as the organizing focus. Here are fifty things to do with your newly available time, energy, and resources. Invite your friends, colleagues, daughters, nieces, and neighbors to join you on this woman-affirming adventure. Be full of yourselves and rock the world!

1. Eat an apple.

2. Breathe!

3. Record the stories of your mothers and grandmothers. Compile them into an anthology.

4. Volunteer at a local nursing home.

5. Write an editorial about the care of seniors in your community.

6. Start an after-school program in your home for the children of single mothers.

7. Find out about your country's first woman scientist.

8. Read the biography of a nineteenth century suffragette.

9. Rent "Bagdad Cafe" and invite your friends over for a Girl's Night Out.  (GNO)

10. ACT UP

11. Plant an apple tree.

12. Go for a long walk and then take a luxurious bath.

13. Read the poems of Phyllis Wheatley.

14. Volunteer as a research-assistant for a woman scholar in your community.

15. Write a poem about your first best friend.

16. Start a "Be Full of Yourself" Club for girls.

17. Find out about your country's first woman doctor.

18. Read the biography of a Queen.

19. Rent "Daughters of the Dust" for a GNO.

20. LOOSEN UP!

21. Bake an apple pie.

22. Create a painting-space in your garage and free the images within you.

23. Read the poems of Sappho.

24. Volunteer at a battered women's shelter.

25. Write a short story about your first job.

26. Co-author a children's book with your grandchildren.

27. Find out about your country's first abortion-rights advocate.

28. Read the biography of a nineteenth century woman-physician.

29. Rent the movie "Antonia's Line" for a GNO.

30. SPEAK UP!

31. Climb an apple tree.

32. Create a meditation-space in your home and nourish the spirit within you.

33. Read the poems of Ntosake Shange.

34. Volunteer as a research-assistant for a woman minister in your community.

35. Write a sermon using all the Scriptural passages referring to God as feminine.

36. Start a school for girls.

37. Find out about your country's first woman minister, priest, or rabbi.

38. Read The Woman's Bible.

39. Rent "Thelma & Louise" for a GNO.

40. LIGHTEN UP!

41. Bob for apples with your women's circle.

42. Create a dance-space in your home and free the movements within you.

43. Read the essays of Audre Lourde.

44. Volunteer as a research-assistant for a feminist physician in your community.

45. Write a song about wearing your first bra.

46. Plan a rite of passage ritual for the adolescent girls.

47. Find out about your country's first woman saxophonist.

48. Read The Creation of Patriarchy.

49. Rent "Fried Green Tomatoes" for a GNO.

50. Bite Into Your Life and the Fullness of Its Possibility!

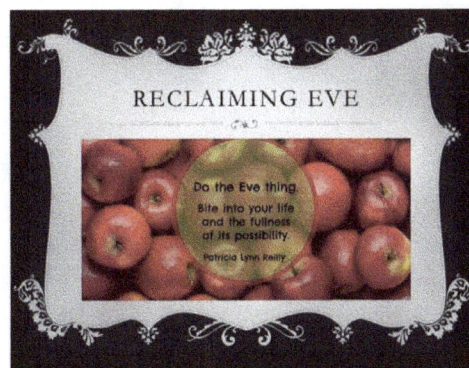

# END NOTES

## Introduction: Words Made Flesh

1. Walt Whitman, *Leaves of Grass*, 1855; "Song of Myself."
2. Chaim Potok, *Davita's Harp*, 1985, Penguin Random House. (The only Potok novel to feature a female protagonist.)
3. UNODC Report: Killings of women and girls by their intimate partner or other family members
   "Globally 81,000 women and girls were killed in 2020, around 47,000 of them (58%) died at the hands of an intimate partner or a family member, which means one woman or girl is being killed every 11 minutes."
   *United Nations Office on Drugs and Crime*
4. Robbie Robertson, *Golden Feather* 1994;
   "When you find out what's worth keeping, with a breath of kindness blow the rest away"

## A Pause Between Introduction and Chapter 1: Clarifying Terms

1. Mona Eltahawy, The Seven Deadly Sin for Women and Girls
2. Annie Laurie Gaylord, Women Without Superstition: No Gods-No Masters; Freedom from Religion Foundation
3. Zoe Marks and Erica Chenoweth, "The Patriarchs' War on Women" (MS. Magazine)

## Chapter 1: A Mighty Revelation

1. bell hooks: "Understanding Patriarchy"
2. Monica Sjoo and Barbara Mor, The Great Cosmic Mother: Rediscovering the Religion of the Earth
3. Queen of Heaven: Jeremiah 7:18 – Cakes for the Queen of Heaven
4. David Biale, "The God with Breasts: El Shaddai in the Bible"; University of Chicago Press Journals
5. JP Nunez, "Why Can Only Men Become Priests?" (The Catholic Exchange)
6. Susan M. Shaw, "How Women in the Southern Baptist Convention Have Fought for Decades to be Ordained" Professor of Women, Gender, and Sexuality Studies, Oregon State University
7. Elizabeth Cady Stanton's essay-turned-book, The Solitude of Self and her co-authored The Woman's Bible are referred to and quoted throughout this book.
8. Gerda Lerner's books The Creation of Patriarchy and The Creation of Feminist Consciousness are referred to and quoted throughout the book.
9. What is Humanism? Humanist Manifesto III

## A Pause Between Chapter 1 and Chapter 2: Clarifying Terms

1. Pallavi Prasad, The Difference Between Sexism and Misogyny, and Why It Matters
2. Elizabeth A. Johnson, Naming God She: The Theological Implications
3. Francine Prose, The Original Sin; Lapham's Quarterly

## Chapter 2: The Genesis Mythology

1. Elizabeth Lesser, Cassandra Speaks: When Women are the Storytellers
2. Miryam Clough, Shame, the Church and the Regulation of Female Sexuality
3. Phyllis Trible, Texts of Terror: Literary-Feminist Readings of Biblical Narratives
4. Christobel Hastings, "God Has Been a Woman Since the Beginning of Time"
5. Merlin Stone, When God was a Woman: Exploration of the Ancient Worship of the Great Goddess

## Chapter 3: A Symposium of Poisonous Words

1. Email patricia@JoinTheReclamation.com to request "A Symposium of Poisonous Words" booklet.

   | Aristotle of Greece | Philo of Alexandria | Paul, the Apostle | Tertullian |
   |---|---|---|---|
   | Augustine | Thomas Aquinas | Martin Luther | Kramer and Sprenger |
   | Rousseau | Sigmund Freud | Karl Barth | Samuel Alito |

2. Emily Jones, The Girl Child's Long Walk to Freedom
3. Pamela Milne, Genesis from Eve's Point of View

### Chapter 4: The Idolatry of God the Father

1. Simone de Beauvoir, The Second Sex
2. Merlin Stone: When God Was a Woman
3. Elinor Gadon, The Once and Future Goddess
4. Origen, Alexandrian Church Father: "What is seen with the eyes of the Creator is Masculine"
5. Steven Roberts, Stanford Professor, How people Visualize God
6. Palladius, The Suicide of Alexandra

### A Pause Between Chapter 4 and Chapter 5

1. Nina Martyris, "Paradise Lost: How The Apple Became The Forbidden Fruit"
2. Rabbi Ari Zivotofsky, "What's the Truth About. . . The Apple in the Garden of Eden?"

### Chapter 5: Eve, Our Mythic Mother

1. Rosemary Radford Ruether, Sexism and God-Talk: Toward a Feminist Theology
2. Epiphanius, The Montanists: They Claim Eve as Their Champion
3. Graves and Patai, Hebrew Myths: The Book of Genesis
4. Sarah Moore Grimke (1792-1873), Feminist Defender of Eve
5. Joanna Southcott (1750-1814), Defender of Bringing Eve's Good Fruit to Humankind
6. Marge Piercy, Applesauce for Eve
7. Women Respond: Contact patricia@JoinTheReclamation.com to request "Outside the Symposium" booklet.

### Chapter 6: Lilith, the Rebellious First Woman

1. Lilith 1, The Lilith Institute
2. Lilith 2, Two Genesis Creation Accounts
3. Elizabeth Cady Stanton, The Woman's Bible and Elizabeth Cady Stanton on Genesis
4. Rosemary Radford Ruether, Sexism and God-Talk: Toward a Feminist Theology
5. Epiphanius: Maximilla, Montanus: Who was the founder of Montanism?
6. Graves and Patai, Hebrew Myths: The Book of Genesis
7. Riane Eisler, The Chalice and the Blade – Partnership Parenting

### A Pause Between Chapter 6 and Chapter 7: Mary's Many Names

1. Nina Martyris, "Paradise Lost: How The Apple Became The Forbidden Fruit"
2. Rabbi Ari Zivotofsky, "What's the Truth About. . . The Apple in the Garden of Eden?"

### Chapter 7: Mary, the Rebellious First Woman

1. Carol Christ: WomanSpirit Rising
2. Mary and Eve: "Six Things to Notice in This Beautiful Image of Mary and Eve" (A Catholic Point of View)
3. Mona Eltahawy, The Seven Necessary Sins
4. Carol Gilligan, How to Dismantle Patriarchy Through Parenting
5. Interfaith Arguments, Protestants Accuse Catholic of Committing Idolatry
6. Marketing Religion, The Pagan Origins of three Catholic Practices

### Chapter 8: Reclaiming Your Original Spirituality

1. Susie Ambrose, Six Ways to Heal from Religious Indoctrination
2. Julia Sweeney, Letting Go of God
3. Marilyn Sewell, Cries of the Spirit
4. Greg M. Epstein, Good Without God: What a Billion Nonreligious People Do Believe

## About the Author

A graduate of Princeton Seminary, Patricia Lynn Reilly's calling as a feminist theologian was inspired by Elizabeth Cady Stanton and her 1898 book *The Woman's Bible* and Gerda Lerner's 1986 book *The Creation of Patriarchy*. Patricia translates the insights of feminism into a language accessible to all women, inspiring (and challenging) them to reclaim their self-sovereignty and to use it to design their lives, love their bodies, and name their own gods. Patricia is also a Humanist Chaplain and a Beginners Eye photographer.

Currently, Patricia serves as Lead Faculty at WomanSpirit Reclamation in partnership with Monette Chilson. Patricia's woman-affirming writings, processes, courses, books, poetry, and songs will be archived at WSR and made available to the women's community in perpetuity, as courses and workbooks, events, circles, and podcasts. www.JoinTheReclamation.com

## Patricia's Books:

- *A God Who Looks Like Me: Discovering a Woman-Affirming Spirituality* (Ballantine Books)
- *Be Full of Yourself: The Journey from Self-Criticism to Self-Celebration* (OWC)
- *Imagine a Woman in Love with Herself: Embracing Your Wholeness and* Wisdom (Conari)
- *I Promise Myself: Making a Commitment to Your Life and Dreams* (Conari)
- *The Women's Empowerment Series:* Six Self-Paced Retreats (IAW International)
- *The Conscious Spirituality* Series (IAW International)
- *A Deeper Wisdom: The 12 Steps from a Woman's Perspective* (WSR, 2020)
- *Love Your Body Regardless: From Body-Judgment to Body-Acceptance* (WSR, 2021)
- *Eve, Our Mythic Mother: Exposing the Lies of Patriarchy* (WSR, 2022)

## About Imagine a Woman International

Patricia founded "Imagine a Woman International" to support the "Imagine a Woman" poem's global distribution. During its active years, IAW International was considered the premiere women's empowerment organization on the planet. The "Imagine a Woman" poem was published in Patricia's first book in 1995. Since then, it has traveled around the world and inspired a global community of women to create woman-affirming books, screenplays, videos, films, works of art, life transitions, professional portfolios, ministries, coaching practices, relationships, and organizational missions.

## About WomanSpirit Reclamation

WSR is an online community of women awakening to their self-sovereignty. Our teachers, guides and facilitators support women as they travel from indoctrination to their own truth. Through virtual gatherings held weekly, monthly and seasonally, we reclaim all that was lost through religious and social systems that excluded women. Join Our Sisterhood

WSR Gatherings: Our regular rhythm includes discussions with authors exploring the many paths to reclamation (In Her Own Words Book Club); sacred services with priestesses and secular guides (Meet Her at the Altar); and weekly support groups that utilize the twelve steps re-written from a woman's perspective by Patricia Lynn Reilly (Wisdom Circles).

WSR Courses: We also take deep dives together in courses designed to illuminate and clear systemic blocks to achieving the self-sovereignty we are working toward in community. These classes include the archetypal reclamation of Eve, Lilith, Sophia and other mythological women in Western culture, as well as the reclamation of self-sovereignty over our bodies, beliefs and lives. Get acquainted with us at www.jointhereclamation.com.

## The "Imagine a Woman" Poem
*Until we imagine something, it remains an impossibility.*
*Once imagined, it becomes our experience.*

Imagine a woman who loves herself. A woman who gazes with loving kindness upon her past and present, body and needs, ideas and emotions. Whose capacity to love deepens as she extends loving kindness to herself.

Imagine a woman who accepts herself. A woman who turns a merciful eye toward her own secrets, successes, and shortcomings. Whose capacity to live non-judgmentally deepens as she is merciful toward herself.

Imagine a woman who participates in her own life with interest and attention. A woman who turns inward to listen, remember, and replenish. Whose capacity to be available deepens as she is available to herself.

Imagine a woman who remains faithful to herself through the seasons of life. A woman who preserves allegiance to herself even when opposed. Whose capacity to remain loyal to others deepens as she is loyal to herself.

Imagine a woman who bites into her own life and the fullness of its possibility. A woman who has opened to the depths of goodness within her. Who affirms the original goodness of her children until the stories of old hold no sway in their hearts.

Imagine a woman who has relinquished the desire for intellectual acceptance and approval. A woman whose authentic words, images, and actions are full of truth and power. Who asserts to herself the right to refashion the world.

Imagine a world where the question "what's wrong with me" has been exorcised from the bodies and lives of our daughters. A world where they cultivate their amazing capacities as children of life. Where they travel a less turbulent path than we did toward self-love, self-acceptance, and self-trust.

Imagine a world where the girl-child's birth is celebrated with as much pomp, circumstance, and opportunity as her brother's; where her body and natural processes are honored without shame and violence; and where she is allowed equal access to its pulpits and altars, thrones, boardrooms, and negotiating tables.

Imagine a community of women who rock the world by giving birth to images of inclusion, poems of truth, rituals of healing, experiences of transformation, relationships of equality, strategies of peace, institutions of justice, and households of compassion for the sake of our children's future. Together, let us imagine into being such a woman, circle, community, and world for the sake of our daughters and sons, and our beloved planet Earth.

You are this woman . . . And so it is.